SELF
BELIEF
is your
SUPER
POWER

Praise for
Self-Belief Is Your Superpower

"One of Australia's top female entrepreneurs and CEOs."
—Nova Entertainment

"A fabulous cheerleader for business owners."
—Melissa Doyle, award-winning journalist

"Tory Archbold is empowering women to realise their potential."
—Channel 7, Australia

"PR and Marketing Powerhouse."
—Money Magazine

"Tory Archbold rose to the top of the cut-throat PR Industry."
—Mamamia

"An absolute powerhouse of a woman."
—Gina DeVee, author of *Audacity to Be Queen*

SELF
BELIEF
is your
SUPER
POWER

Unleash Your Life Purpose
Own Your Power
Become a Magnet for Miracles

Tory Archbold

Founder + Creator of Powerful Steps

mango
PUBLISHING GROUP
CORAL GABLES

Cover Design: Roberto Núñez
Interior Illustrations: Elena/stock.adobe.com
Layout & Design: Megan Werner

For permission requests, please contact the publisher at:
Mango Publishing Group
2850 S Douglas Road, 2nd Floor
Coral Gables, FL 33134 USA
info@mango.bz

For special orders, quantity sales, course adoptions and corporate sales, please email the publisher at sales@mango.bz. For trade and wholesale sales, please contact Ingram Publisher Services at customer.service@ingramcontent.com or +1.800.509.4887.

Self-Belief Is Your Superpower: Unleash Your Life Purpose, Own Your Power, and Become a Magnet for Miracles

Library of Congress Cataloging-in-Publication number: 2022950391
ISBN: (p) 978-1-68481-156-4 (e) 978-1-68481-157-1
BISAC category code: BUS109000, BUSINESS & ECONOMICS / Women in Business

Printed in the United States of America

I believe in the magic of everyday miracles and would like to thank three of mine.

To my darling daughter, Isabella Jane. You are a miracle I could not live without. You have taught me about love, truth, and compassion, and I am so proud of the woman you are today and the woman you will become tomorrow.

To my incredible husband. I thank my lucky stars that the universe conspired to bring us together. You believed in the magic of us, and I believe in the magic of you.

To the challenges faced along the highway of life—thank you. It's been one hell of a crazy ride and without them, I would not be here today.

Much love,
TORY xoxo

The Roadmap Forward

Introduction_____9

CHAPTER ONE
**Build a Life from Zero
to Hero with Self-Belief**_____13

CHAPTER TWO
**Unleashing Your
Life's Purpose**_____25

CHAPTER THREE
The Power of Dreams_____41

CHAPTER FOUR
**How to Feed Your Soul
and Create Miracles**_____59

CHAPTER FIVE
**Attract the Right Partners with
a Powerful Personal Brand**_____73

CHAPTER SIX
**Coffee, Not Lunch:
The Power of Connection**_____89

CHAPTER SEVEN
The Art of Delegation_____99

CHAPTER EIGHT
Delivering Global Impact_____115

CHAPTER NINE
Be True to You_____139

CHAPTER TEN
**Nothing Is Perfect:
Success vs. Survival**_____149

CHAPTER ELEVEN
Culling Your Tribe_____161

CHAPTER TWELVE
**Stepping into Your Power
Zone and Finding
Your Purpose**_____179

CHAPTER THIRTEEN
Total Alignment_____197

CHAPTER FOURTEEN
Your Next Powerful Step_____213

Offer Pages_____218

Acknowledgments_____223

About the Author_____227

Introduction

A *happy heart is a magnet for miracles.* The power of these words transformed my life and they are about to transform yours. Make them your daily mantra as they are an energy mindset that will empower you to live life on your own terms, delivering the ultimate power you can give yourself: to love *you* from the inside out. When you live with freedom in your heart, you will attract abundance the right way. You will not fear judgment and will not be afraid to stand up and be proud of who you are. You will be able to show up and understand the power of a mutual exchange of energy to showcase your *value* to others so that you are seen, heard, and can make a difference in a world we all call home.

For two decades, I have reshaped brands, businesses, and lives using the proven strategies in this book, which have been developed working with entrepreneurs, CEOs, and the most recognized Fortune 500 brands worldwide. This book has been created to show you a pathway to plot your own personal roadmap to success, to become your own success story and lead from the heart.

You will come to learn that one coffee date can change your life, and that the power of leaning into your own story and the stories of others will allow you to switch your thinking to level up and know that anything in this lifetime is possible—because it is.

SELF-BELIEF IS YOUR SUPERPOWER

I will show you how to trust your intuition, step into your power, and break free of judgment by igniting your ultimate superpower: your self-belief.

The gift you can give to yourself while reading is to trust the process, as these insights will drive change in your life, the lives of those you lead, and those you choose to surround yourself with. And yes, this involves making some hard decisions you may have put off about which future road you want to walk down, as evolution only comes from stepping outside of your comfort zone to find your power zone.

The power of game-changing moments shared from the many incredible women in our community is what lights me up, so do not be afraid to share your wins from reading this book. When they have a win, they share it, and seeing this story on social media from Alice Almeida is one of them. It sets the tone for what you will learn because when you believe you can, you will.

"I have been trying to secure an interview with this incredible fertility professor based in the US for over twelve months. I am massively intimidated by his intelligence, so I have emailed only. After a few follow up emails and no response, I decided to give up until I met Tory Archbold via her Powerful Steps program. If you have witnessed Tory in action, you will understand when I say this woman has really stepped into, and owns, her power. She is not scared or intimidated to ask the tough questions, and she goes after what she wants with this strength and determination that I am in awe of. I wouldn't be surprised if her next coffee date is with Michelle Obama!

"So a few weeks ago, I thought 'What would Tory do?' and I called the professor's office. I spoke with his assistant, left a message about interviewing him, AND HE CALLED BACK!!! I'm interviewing him in a few weeks' time and I am completely scared shi...pless!!

"So why am I sharing this? Well, one of the learnings from the Powerful Steps program was 'So what if they say no?'

"I had this fear of no, and I let it stop me from trying. So now, I will make every decision with a 'What if they say yes?' mentality.

"So—ask that question! They actually might say yes!

"Maybe I'll ask Michelle Obama for coffee?! Ha, kidding. Baby steps..."

With Alice's story in mind, let's start this next adventure of life together.

Much love, and always remember to dream BIG.

TORY xox

PS: Michelle, let's have a coffee date!

CHAPTER ONE

Build a Life from Zero to Hero with Self-Belief

"I can and I will."

—Tory Archbold

There is magic within each one of us. The trick to finding it is to find yourself. Tapping into this magic, I started my first business at twenty-four, attracting the world's top-performing brands, celebrities, and influencers. I built a team of twenty-two. I was not degree educated. I was educated through the power of connection, and along the way, I never said to myself, "This is hard," or "I can't do this." I always said to myself, "I want to work with the best of the best, which means I need to be the best of the best"—and to be the best of the best, you must be agile and believe in possibilities. You must have an open heart and an open mind, but most importantly, you must understand what's going on in the world and how you can add value to deliver impact and lead others.

Success is within us, too. It simply waits for that powerful moment when it nudges us through an unexpected challenge or life experience. To create success, we must understand our soul's purpose and align our frequency with the direction we wish to pursue. The first powerful step we can take is to give ourselves permission to lean into what truly lights us up and ignites the fire that completes us both in business and in life. Achieving balance with purpose is a tough gig, as we can achieve great success in one part of our life and feel we are failing in another. When you crack the code and understand your life purpose, you will be given the role of conduit holding a privileged space for others to rise. To pay forward your life experiences in this "role" is known as a "gift" and through the power of storytelling, you can show others that challenges in life will always become possibilities no matter the circumstances they face. By owning your life journey and stepping into your power by taking ownership of your powerful story, you will learn to trust and follow the signs of life. Synchronicities will magically appear, and you will find contentment because you are living with purpose. What bothered you in your past will not be taken into your future because you became the warrior princess who broke free from the shackles holding you back.

This book is written from the heart, based on learnt experiences to empower you to claim your own ultimate self by unleashing self-belief and internal happiness so that you become a magnet for miracles through an understanding that the lens you choose to view life through will become your ultimate asset. The lessons we learn along the highway of life are hard but necessary to discover what triggers us by digging deep within our souls to reveal the number-one gift we were born with (insert happy dance here). With this powerful mindset in your tool kit, every dream you ever had will become your ultimate reality. I know this to be true because it is my everyday reality.

The power of possibility becomes clear when you understand the power of self-belief. When you allow self-belief to become your superpower, it will deliver miracles as you recognize that what finds us grows us. If we believe we can, we will. There is always a way forward—life is that simple, if you strip back the clutter and distractions holding you back. Rock bottom is not a bad place to be. As I like to say to others when they are at a crossroads in life, if you're uncomfortable with where you are, take yourself back to a moment in time you may be struggling to accept, and ask if you would do things differently. If the answer is yes, you have work to do, and if it's not, then you're on track to move forward. When you are in the position to move forward, you will find yourself in a position of service to others where you will have the ability to create and deliver impact. Always honor that this is often a temporary gift of leadership and may not be your forever "role." So, while it is, make an impact—lead from the heart, disrupt, and most importantly, make a difference in the lives of those who surround you. You might have seen on social media feeds the saying, "Be that woman who fixes another's crown without telling them it was crooked." This will be you.

By learning how to be present and in the moment, you will always be able to rise—it's how you choose to rise by empowering others that will make what you have to offer different. Think of it as empathetic disruptive leadership, the ability to shift people's perceptions and mindsets for the better. As you rise, never forget where you came from. It gave you the foundation to be you, the "conduit" leaning into the power of your life purpose—your how, your why, the advocacy that presents itself when the timing is right to propel you forward to heights you may not have thought possible. With a clear understanding and acceptance of who you are, you will not be defined by others' limited thoughts or expectations, and this will set you apart in business and in life. From a place of trust within yourself, you will learn that you are capable of anything in this lifetime. You have the inner strength to tap into self-belief by understanding your path and being unafraid to walk it. This is your ultimate gift and the ultimate opportunity to step up and live a life by design while being of service to others. Are you ready to fly with me on the journey of a lifetime?

My career started with rejection. When everyone said, "No, you can't do that," I said, "Yes, I can" and never questioned my ability to create a dream business that would deliver a global impact because I anchored every one of my thoughts when building that business to the facts I knew by visualizing and manifesting the outcome. These facts became my "go-to" in life and helped me to rise. I loved the power of people and how they could make a difference in the world through leadership, brand, and consumer experiences. It lit me up from the inside out, and I wanted to play a part in that world, make a difference, start a business, create, and deliver extraordinary and memorable experiences—the type people never forget. I wanted the ability to travel the world and take in new experiences, so I positioned myself at the heartbeat of an industry I loved. I mapped out the brands I wanted to work with, the people I admired, and the countries I wanted to visit, and I anchored my decisions back to the facts of *why* I was creating this business. *How* I would build the business came through the power of connection and partnership, a global network of referrals, and the advocacy created anchored to my value set created momentum. I learnt to trust life's flow and surrendered to these two facts:

1. There is always a reason people find you, and you never know who is watching your moves. Never give up.

2. Believe in the power of what you are creating, and, as it gains momentum, you will know you are on track.

I recognized through momentum I could not grow alone and that was when team investment and mentors who pushed me outside of my comfort zone became the greatest asset for growth. The advocacy started flowing into my life from synchronicity because I was invested in the power of connection and people. From a CEO meeting, a coffee date connection in a New York nightclub and then flew to Sydney to appoint us for a global brand launch; to a high street retailer in London tracking me down in Paris to launch their brand in Australia, these opportunities came for a reason and a purpose. Most importantly, they came because of the energy and momentum behind my *why* and *how*. To this day and through the practice of gratitude, the power of advocacy and connection to life shows me my purpose. It shows me how to move forward and I 100 percent trust that process. From a Koh Samui breakfast date with a US connection, who "happened" to be neighbors with a supermodel I interviewed on my podcast in Los Angeles, I have learnt that relationships are built because of the magic of miracles and synchronicity, and there is a reason why the universe brings us together. These synchronicities are no coincidence and are built with purpose because we are on the highway of life together, and we are here to help each other thrive.

I'm a big believer in human connection to build a powerful network and a commitment to three coffee dates a week throughout my career has built trust, loyalty, and advocacy. Ironically rejection over a coffee date built my career. When I returned from London after completing the working holiday visa in my early twenties, I started having three coffee dates a week: one with someone in my tribe, one with someone I wanted to partner with, and one with someone completely outside my comfort zone. I was sitting at Bills in Sydney, and my coffee date was with a man I trusted with all my heart. I said, "I would like to start a media communications agency, and I would like to partner with the world's top-performing brands, celebrities and influencers. I'm going to start this agency in Australia, and I'm going to take it global."

He looked at me and said, "Why would you want to do that?"

To which I replied, "Because I can."

I had fallen in love with storytelling during my time in London, where I'd had the opportunity to work with the best of the best: Viacom, Columbia TriStar, and George Lucas Films on the working holiday visa, which was the training ground for what I wanted to achieve in my career. So, I asked him, "Why do you think I can't do this?"

And he said, "Well, I think you are best suited to go and complete your interior design degree, get married, have those three children, join a few clubs, and just live your best life."

I remember walking out of that coffee date, and something inside of me unleashed its power. I had an aha moment, thinking, "I'm going to do this." I knew creating this business was my calling, and I was sick of being placed in a box of standard expectations. All he did was repeat what my family always told me, and it made me feel like I wasn't good enough for anything beyond those expectations. Crazy, right? I know now we are all good enough to create and chase dreams, and I thank them every day for those limited beliefs that delivered my first powerful step toward creating a business. I would build powerful brands for others on my own terms.

Despite having zero money in my bank account and no media connections, I backed myself and registered TORSTAR. The journey began with the assets I did have—passion, integrity, and the ability to deliver. I landed my first client through rejection, too. Nobody in Australia believed I could create this business, so I reached out to my network in London, and the first miracle appeared. It was a connection to the number-one retailer in Australia. They believed in what I could offer, and I signed my first client.

When you are stepping into your power, you learn quickly that every challenge you are presented with becomes an opportunity and you find a solution. I was given a role as an assistant at MTV Europe by learning to type as I knew it would provide the opportunity to work with the best of the best in media in the '90s. Without any writing or media experience, I created a press release to land my first marque client for TORSTAR. Wanting to develop relationships with global retailers, I took myself around the world and learnt how the best shopping experiences operated so I could speak the language of the people who ran them. When online shopping was introduced to consumers and the world's best became my clients, I was an avid experiential shopper. I wanted to understand the nuts and bolts of how online worked from a consumer perspective and the backend processes that delivered that experience. When we worked with high-profile celebrities, I knew they were people with everyday feelings just like you and me. They experienced tough times, but due to the nature of their polished public-facing brands, they were not allowed to speak about how tough that journey was as they were locked into the profile others had built for them. They were the "money maker" in a business that drove sales, and often they were surrounded by teams of "enablers" who were afraid to say no and didn't want to hear about their tough times. I had a different approach, placing myself in their shoes by researching what was going on in their lives and how I could help bring out the best in them for the brand they were representing, and was never afraid of the word "no." If it didn't feel right, I chose not to do it.

Challenges and experiences inspired me. They kept me motivated in business as I gained knowledge that others were not willing to learn. I was a risk-taker and knew that if I levelled up, I would attract the next level up. I was always riding the wave of momentum and found it hard to step off, until my world came crashing down and I had to reconfigure my life after surviving a near-death experience, which meant realignment. I had become that hardworking woman, available to everyone except myself. My guess is that you may have been that woman too.

I believe we have two journeys in life: the before and after. Chapter one—my before—set me up for who I am today; it laid the foundation for the next chapter and showed me another way to "do life" and gave me purpose on a whole new vibrational level. I saw the gaps in my life, and I wanted to fill them up with love, happiness, and joy, which meant I had to learn personal lessons on repeat until I was ready to level up and own them. Those were tough times but I know we all go through challenges in different stages of our lives and in different formats. How we choose to take ownership of our part in the "play of our life" is what sets us apart from the pack. The more I am open and honest about that time of my life, the more opportunities I am given to help others going through that same transformational moment. My role is to pick them up and show them the possibilities of embracing change by shining a light, so they know it's OK—it will work out, and there will be the next-level version of *them*. When I started this second chapter of my life—my after—I made a promise to myself. You can call it a "manifestation." It was a simple statement: "I will attract those who operate at a high vibration. My role will be to take them higher, so they deliver impact by owning the power of their story." I said "high vibration" because these women were just like you—they already had success; they just weren't aware of their power to claim it because the common thread was being at a crossroads on the road of life. This is your calling and the best time to invest in deciding which highway is the next journey to drive down to live your best life and with whom you choose to share it.

Do you fear change? You are not alone. Everyone has a fear, including the world's greatest leaders, celebrities, and influencers. Fear is universal and can involve fear of change, judgment, failure, rejection, uncertainty, getting hurt, loneliness, or the fear that you will never ever be loved. To become fearless, you need to acknowledge your fear, step into it, use positive self-talk, get comfortable with being uncomfortable, break habits by becoming braver in your everyday decision-making, and, most importantly, embrace failure. Failure is seen as life's greatest teacher. When we stop being afraid of failure and accept it, we can dream and think big because we realize that every experience, good or bad, teaches us something. I love failure because it teaches me new, exciting ways to live and embrace life.

Knowing this, our greatest challenge becomes our greatest asset. The challenges we face are always sent as secret nudges for us to level up to the next stage of our careers or help us release energy blocks that are holding us back from finding total fulfillment. The greater the challenge, the greater the leap forward, and, when you start viewing the gift of the challenge as a power move forward, you will begin to see that everyday miracles surround you. While there is no magic wand for happiness, nor a secret wand to get you to the top of your game in business, there is a miracle wand you can give yourself, and it will become your superpower. It's called self-belief, and, if my teenage daughter can utilize this success mindset, so can you.

In her final two years at school, she decided to back herself with no learnt skill set or example of success by singing in French to secure her final marks for graduation. She gave up perfectly good marks in other subjects and was unwavering in knowing she would succeed. I knew she had a great voice from the many road trips we went on, singing at the top of our voices, living in the moment, loving life, and giving it our all. For the record, I am a terrible singer, but I could see this passion in her and knew if she invested in herself and her dream there was a possibility she would succeed and she did. We watched her stand up and sing in front of her school in a way that brought tears to other people's eyes, and in that moment, I knew that no matter what success she attracts in life, this was her defining moment. She believed she could, she did, and her final year results matched her intuition—she was a top thirty performer in the state.

If you're ready for change, you will understand that these four signposts signify the time is right for you to make your move, try something different, explore new opportunities, and embrace the next chapter of your life.

1.   **Your motivation is gone and you're thinking, "What's next?"** It feels like your journey has come full circle and you're

struggling to find passion in your job, relationship, or friendship group. Take it as a sign that you're about to step into another level of life.

2. **Feeling bored?** Boredom breeds lethargy. As humans, we need stimulation in our daily lives. Otherwise, we can feel scared, stressed, and unhappy. If you can tell that you no longer have that stimulation in your life, then it's a sign you're ready for a change.

3. **Feeling stressed?** If you're constantly under stress, your body will nudge you to slow down by showing physical symptoms. For me, this always shows up as a swollen stomach and being asked if I am pregnant. For you, this could be headaches, an upset stomach, high blood pressure, chest pain, problems with sex, or restless sleep. Stress leads to emotional problems, depression, and panic attacks, but it's something we can all avoid by tackling the hard stuff and owning who we are and what we want from life.

4. **Feeling scared?** It's perfectly normal to fear change because an outcome is unknown. Our brains are designed to find peace in knowing. When we don't know what will happen, our brains trick us into making "what if" scenarios, and we find it hard to move on when something known comes to an end.

By embracing these feelings, you will feel uncomfortable. It also means you're ready to hustle and become ready to do the things other people won't do. You will do them with joy and purpose because you love them. Stepping into that next-level version of you will provide you with experience. It can help you learn lessons. It will open doors that might otherwise be closed. The good news is you will feel empowered when you step up and take ownership of who you are, and that, my beautiful friend, is called a powerful step!

THREE POWERFUL BUSINESS MANTRAS TO TRANSLATE A DREAM INTO REALITY:

◇ *Keep going, keep believing; you can because you will.*

◇ *Step into your power, stay in your lane, and compare yourself to no one.*

◇ *By claiming my power, I will align with my destiny and always wake up with a happy heart.*

Be sure to download your daily mantras from me in your digital bonuses at selfbeliefisyoursuperpower.com/bonus.

CHAPTER TWO

Unleashing Your Life's Purpose

"We all have a choice—we can watch things happen or step into our power and make things happen. I choose to make them happen, and that's a powerful affirmation to propel you forward in business and in life."

—Tory Archbold

Want to know a fun fact?

I am not degree educated and built both of my businesses through the power of connection and self-belief. Sure, some people didn't believe in me, but I chose to believe in myself. I believe we are only limited by other people's limited imaginations. Always dream *big* and never be afraid to reach for the stars. Identify what you want. Create a journal where you want to take that dream and shift your energy forward by taking powerful steps toward achieving it. I still have the journal I wrote in to create TORSTAR and it's a daily reminder that dreams come true.

If you find flow you find purpose. Purpose is a gift from birth that guides and sustains us and is the reason why we can live a life in complete alignment deep within our heart and soul. It's your *why* and is essential for living a happy, healthy, fulfilled life, your get up and *go*, your everyday aha moment knowing you are on the right track living life to your greatest and fullest potential. Some people know their purpose right away; others take time to figure it out. I found it clicked into total alignment in my forties. It wasn't that I didn't have a life purpose prior; it was just that what I was stepping into felt different, it felt right, it felt easy, and it was a feeling of total alignment as everyday miracles started appearing in my life. I took those miracles as a sign I had arrived at the crossroads in life when you need a new runway and was 110 percent ready to embrace it. I never questioned this new runway; I just knew that the right opportunities and the right people would find me because my purpose was an energy match and trusted the process simply because I had removed what was no longer serving me to live in flow, in my power and aligned with the exciting new future runway that had presented itself.

In my TORSTAR days, my intent and purpose was to create and build powerful brands. Stepping into Powerful Steps, it was to inspire, encourage, and empower others in the entrepreneurial and business space by taking ownership of who they are so they could discover their unique gift and showcase it to the world adding value to the lives of others. TORSTAR gave me the global experience and networks to develop a unique skill set that could then be transferred into a higher vibrational way of doing business for those at a crossroads in their life simply because I had been that person and had lived experience others could lean into. I had experienced incredible career highs but most importantly had learnt some tough lessons and worked hard to navigate breakthroughs transforming challenges into opportunities. Those years of success and survival aligned me to my purpose of writing this book, being here with you today, joining you on that next exciting journey along your highway of life, the one in which you desire to operate in flow and alignment, the one where you can attract what you deserve if you are willing to become present to the everyday miracles that surround you that you may not currently see. We will explore possibilities to fuse your life purpose professionally and personally with a powerful tool kit to unleash your superpower in the chapters ahead. I've lived and learnt from this tool kit; it is my secret life weapon, and the time has come to share it with you.

Stepping into your power and purpose takes practice. Practice in the sense that you will fail a lot. When I started my agency, it was clear I needed to present to people to earn their respect when I pitched an idea, concept, or campaign. Business and connection do not get "given to you"; it gets "gifted" as a mutual exchange of energy to achieve a desired outcome and I was on a steep learning curve. I was good at delivering the outcome as each brand we won referred to another, but I wanted to get better at the delivery of how I presented myself, so I looked up online speaking courses that gave you the confidence to speak with high-level executives and audiences in an open forum. When I was in my late twenties, I knew this was a life skill that would take me far if I nailed the basics and decided on a two-day group course hosted by Larry Edmur, a TV personality known as an asset to media networks in Australia. In those early days of business, I loved watching how others operated and told the power of their brand stories; the presentations we did were usually to small groups of people, not the level I wanted to step into on a global scale to attract the brands on my manifestation board. So, I had to learn how to show up in a new and exciting way, which meant I had to "show up" and present. I was not brave, fearless, and courageous like I am today; instead I was self-conscious and just plain awful due to a fear of stepping into the unknown. Larry had placed me outside of my comfort zone on day one, and his role was to place me into my power zone, which I kept stuffing up as I was so nervous in a room full of strangers. On day two something inside of me shifted, and I found my ultimate purpose for making this investment in my career and owned it. I had to break through the unknown and just go for it—I stopped panicking, stepped into the moment, owned who I was, and never looked back. I now speak on stage to thousands of people, sharing the power of my story, and it started from being present in that room, with Larry, believing in the number-one reason I was there, blasting me off in a whole new career direction with confidence, grace, and gratitude.

The first powerful step toward finding your purpose is to find out what drives and energizes you, because there will be times in your career when you say to yourself, "Am I willing to invest time in this as it's not setting my heart on fire anymore?" That's OK as it's just a shift of focus and your intuition telling you that chapter of your life is over and a new one is beginning to emerge. Crazy as it sounds, when this shift was happening toward the end of the journey with TORSTAR I could never get a car park at my office despite paying for two of them. Someone was always blocking me from coming to work because they had decided that they were entitled to my spot rather than finding or paying for one. I would get so frustrated with the process of the everyday fight: tracking down the owner of the car, explaining this was marked as private parking, and saying "Please appreciate that, as a business, we're losing valuable hours I could be investing in my team and clients. So please, can you not do this again?" Of course, they always did, and I decided to recognize that energy block, work from home more often, and delegate to the team as the universe clearly did not want me in the office five days a week focused on this business and was preparing my next move—to downsize for new beginnings and a more balanced life.

I recognized that downsizing and creating space for what I wanted needed to happen by acknowledging what was no longer serving me (like the car park energy zappers) allowed me to feel lighter and brighter when I released my attention to that trigger point and the universal laws of attraction. Giving it no attention and making myself unavailable to the takers gave me back the energy I was lacking, and I began to clearly see that if I committed to major change, a more purposeful path forward could appear at the crossroads in which I was standing. I had been single for close to a decade while building a global business and raising my daughter alone; the timing felt right to shake things up. I decided to serve myself first by exploring what I was willing to sacrifice versus whom and what I chose to share my life with. To gain clarity on these thoughts meant I needed space to think. The first powerful step I took forward was to delegate more to my team empowering them to step up and deliver while I worked through my thought process, discovering my new life purpose and what this transformation could look like. Giving yourself space means clearing your diary to address the triggers holding you back and taking ownership of the good, the bad, and the ugly to remove the clouds that are forming so that you only see sunlight. It is what I call non-negotiable "me time."

Letting go of our iconic showroom and office space along with the frustrating car park scenario that triggered me daily all of a sudden seemed easy. I made the decision to downsize the team with new premises, choosing only to work with clients and brands that were 100 percent in alignment with my values—and it felt good! As my business grew over the years, we had senior executives who had secured brands I didn't like because of the toxic energy attached to the people who ran them. I didn't care if they were high-profile and influential; the energy match wasn't right, and they were the first brands I called to say, "We are not the agency for you and here is my recommended way forward for your brand to ensure you have continued success." I did this with grace and style anchoring my decision-making to my value set as I knew nobody likes to hear that an agency doesn't want to work with you. It was about rewiring how I had let others step into my business and taking that ownership back to bring it into alignment with what worked for me, not against me. I could feel the energy shift with each powerful move forward, decluttering my business model as I leaned into the feeling that my life purpose was cheering me on from the inside out.

Feeling brave, powerful, and exhilarated by creating space for discovery was a game-changer, and I followed these four simple steps to focus my thoughts on *how, why,* and if *I am truly ready* to embrace a changed thought process.

Lean into the power of this simple exercise and see what is revealed to you.

1. Why do I do the things I do?

2. What drives me?

3. What am I missing?

4. What impact do my choices have on the life I want?

For me, the answer was clear as I worked through each question, defining my reasoning, challenging myself, and being raw and real about what I valued and could do without until I arrived at the answer—which was yes! I was ready to embrace change and my intent was clear for the universe: "Show me how so that I can follow the signs and seek the answers to step into my truth and destiny."

In 2017, Bella thought it would be fun to go to Las Vegas for New Year's Eve together, and I remember thinking, "OK, I am prepared to dance with teenagers at midnight," yet she surprised me with her choice of Celine Dion at Caesars Palace, as I couldn't imagine many teenagers dancing to Celine. I could imagine Celine bringing the power of her words and energy to millions around the world to manifest their true intent for the new year. The stage was set, and we were in prime seats. We knew the words and were prepared for the magic of new beginnings. Those twenty-four hours in Vegas changed my life because my intent and purpose became clear—I wished for "love and adventure," and the magic of miracles in 2018 delivered above and beyond my wildest dreams—I had cleared the deck for new beginnings. Miracles are phenomena that defy logical reasoning and seem impossible but happen anyway. I know miracles happen as a fact of life, which is why you are reading this book, wanting to discover how they can find you too. My life's miracle was about to find its way to us without me even knowing it was happening until boom: everything I had ever hoped and dreamed for gave me the happiest heart I could ever imagine.

When you're on the highway of life you want to have the right tribe by your side as it's a key part of taking ownership of who you are and what you want in life. You should never "settle" for the wrong family, friends, or clients because of obligation. That's a lot of space you want to clear of negativity and replace with positivity, so that you can fly high and enjoy every moment you have been gifted on this planet. Your foundational tribe will always remind you of the power of unconditional love and be there for you for the highs, the lows, and the game-changing moments that will keep coming for you as part of your growth strategy. These people are pivotal in preparing you for change and supporting you as you dive deep **to make the power moves to embrace change**. You will find yourself in a special portal when you are ready to surrender to this process and receive miracles meant for you.

I was in that very portal, and this is what happened next. I knew my business would take care of itself while I focused on my NYE resolution for "love and adventure," and I also knew I was not afraid of judgment. So I hopped online by deep diving into the world of "dating" for the very first time of my life and joining Bumble at LAX with my daughter. My intent was clear—I was ready to share my life with my soulmate and I wanted her on the journey as if I was going to bring love into "our life"—I wanted to be 100 percent in alignment with what made us both happy. This was important to me, as she had missed the opportunity to experience family life in her formative years due to our circumstances (more on that later). So we thought about the approach like this: we had been watching How to Lose a Guy in Ten Days on repeat during our vacation, thanks to the limited number of movies available for a twelve-year-old to watch in a hotel room and decided to switch our thinking. What if I could win a guy in less than a week? I didn't have ten days I could solely dedicate to dating, but I did have time to go on five dates in six days and see what unfolded. So, we anchored my profile to my truth: global traveler, business owner, and mama of one with recent images we both liked from our trip. I discovered when we landed fifteen hours later that I was an online dating novice who couldn't date a man who lived over 12,000 kilometers away in another country, which meant I had to swipe right again!

When you step into your intent and purpose, you have to ensure there is room for a few U-turns, which means a thorough process of discovery and being truthful to your brand when you decide to step outside of your comfort zone and commit to meeting new people. I had always been afraid a client would see me on a dating app, so I avoided dating to remain professional, but I discovered this was the "new norm" in the world of matchmaking. I learnt more about myself on those five dates in six days than I had in years and will share these learnings with you to know that no matter what stage of life you are in, you can grow, learn, and evolve too.

- **Do not judge.** One guy offered to pick me up on a moped. I had never been on one before and was wary, so I said, "Stuff it, I'm trying something new," and he turned out to be a CEO of an ASX-listed company who was sick of women wanting his money and lifestyle, so this was his way of trying to find "the one" by arriving in a mode of transport he loved and seeing the reaction.

- **Everyone has a story.** One guy took me for dinner and asked where I had spent our family Christmas. I explained my situation and said it was just my daughter and me. We had a great time having lunch at a hotel in Santa Monica on the beach and then went for a bike ride in an area we were considering moving to. I asked, "How was yours?"

He said, "I don't really like my family and had to smoke a spliff to relax me before I saw them to deal with the day." Now this man judged me for not wanting to spend time with my family at Christmas because I had chosen to remove us from a toxic situation, and we were happy living life on our own terms. Who's the person in their power? Me owning that fact or him having to take drugs to cope with it and not be in alignment with his true authentic feelings? It was a "no" from me for a second date.

- **Some people want to control you.** The next guy seemed nice. We knew a few of the same people and went out on a couple of dates, which came to a grinding halt when he asked, "Why haven't you kissed or slept with me yet? You're a single mum, and don't you want financial stability?" Um, no thanks. I can provide that for myself.

- **Always stand in your truth.** I dated one of those stereotypical guys who worked in banking and realized I couldn't pretend I was happy. I was not prepared to compromise on what I wanted from a relationship, and my choice was to be happy and treated as an equal. He arrived at my house with his dirty laundry on a Thursday night as he was going away to Hong Kong for the weekend, and I guess he wanted to prepare himself for the next week. We had seen each other eight or nine times over two months, and before we went for dinner he said, "I'll be back Sunday night. Can you dry-clean my clothes?" And I thought, "Is he going to give me some money or is he just expecting me to drop off his laundry and pay for it?" I realized that was what he expected me to do, and that was the end of that—I'm not a housekeeper nor a woman after a few dinner dates and a 60 percent compatibility rate who does your dirty laundry. Nor am I going to settle for second best.

I had learnt the art of surrender and following the signs, so while I was disappointed those five dates didn't work out, I learnt something about myself and what I valued, which was the gift I had been given. Just because something doesn't work out doesn't mean you can't try again. So, I did, I tried again, and the stars aligned in so many ways because I followed the signs and trusted myself to operate outside of my comfort zone. I'm not a pub kind of woman, yet I met my husband on a Bumble date at a pub. Before he arrived, they were playing toss the boss for drinks, and I was asked to pick heads or toes. I picked heads and won. There were so many synchronicities between us, and we just clicked. We met in May, yet the turning point for both of us was a few months prior on March 22, 2018. He had just completed a major project he was passionate about, and I had been sitting on a beach in Thailand and at that exact moment had written in my journal, "I am free to be me and trust each moment as I am miraculously happy and content." We were both happy and content in our own skins, thousands of miles apart, and the universe conspired to bring us together. We did not have one mutual friend; we received a miracle, and I would not have stepped into the woman I am today without him as he is everything I ever wanted and more.

So how did we receive that energy match? My husband believes it was through learning valuable lessons and every experience he gained made him stronger, empowering him to identify what he really wanted. As he explains, "There is no silver bullet to finding happiness." He had to shift his way through life lessons to align all the parts to find his true purpose and passion. When working on his passion, his energy shifted, and life became enjoyable, which placed him in a good head space. When you're in a good space you can attract and keep high vibrational experiences, so the opportunities he attracted were bigger and better for all the right reasons, which I know made him ready for "us."

Finding your purpose and true life meaning takes patience and time. Nothing ever happens overnight—what you can do to shift the energy forward is let go of the past. By learning to surrender and let go of your fears, you become more receptive to new opportunities. I have witnessed many women struggle and hold onto their past. Here are some easy wins to shift your energy to reconcile your past, attract the unconditional love you may seek in your future, or level up in business and life.

- **Don't take your problems to bed.** Leave them at the door. Remove anything related to the challenge you are facing out of this sacred, energetic space as your body energetically heals itself while you sleep. This includes removing paperwork related to a negative situation or the bed you shared with an ex-partner. Remove it or sell it. That is the old you, and your bedroom energy should only be used as a space for the new you.

- **Do not wear the energy of a failed relationship.** It's done and dusted. Let it go. There is no need to wear an engagement ring on your finger from a failed marriage. It takes that negative experience and energy forward and shows the world you are incapable of letting go or moving on.

- **Invest in self-care.** Spend time healing in nature, go for long walks, and shift how you invest in yourself. All it takes is a diary block and switching off your phone. Become available to yourself as nature is the greatest healer and producer of miracles. Slowing down allows you to become more aware of life's simplicity, anchoring you to receive what is meant for you. Become present and aware of a flower, laughter, raindrops. There is magic all around you, if you are willing to open yourself to new beginnings and a happy heart.

- **Listen to a high-vibe song—on repeat!** Try SUPER HI and Neeka's "Following the Sun," as the words are perfect for transformation and motivation: "Wanna chase a miracle? It's possible. You just gotta open the door"—meaning give yourself permission to try something new because it may surprise you.

For my husband, finding his purpose happened organically and it was down to "trial and error" on what did and did not make him happy, where he found his passion and where he didn't. He moved from a corporate role and ventured into setting up his own business, which he thought would make him happy. One day he bumped into someone from his corporate life and was instantly drawn to the conversation and the relationships he had built up in an industry he loved. He realized he wasn't in alignment with his passion and purpose with the business he had set up, acknowledging what he was doing wasn't an energy match. It took time to figure out and empower himself to secure the right role for his return to a corporate role and this came through the power of his connections and the conversations that reignited his passion for what set his heart on fire. He trusts the process of change and loves what he does—it lights him up, driving his purpose, as he knows he is creating value while serving others.

A fun fact about our relationship? When I met him, I intended to move to Santa Monica with my daughter to set up another business, as I was ready for new beginnings. The universe had other plans as we fell in love in Australia and our children were educated there. When he set his intention to marry me, he sent a photo of a diamond he liked and asked what I thought about the energy as he knows I love leaning into "good energy" when making decisions. I immediately loved it and said, "Let's fly over to pick it up," thinking it would be in Singapore or Hong Kong. Without him knowing, the diamond he chose was in LA, and every day I wear the energy of his love on my wedding finger. I am reminded that he captured the miracle available to us and fused our energy with intention, love, and purpose, and who knows, maybe we will live in LA one day and make another dream a reality, too!

Trusting the process means you must trust yourself. Your purpose will find you when you understand and acknowledge the power of you. One of the questions I am asked the most on social media is, "How did you know what you wanted to do?" It's simple: I followed the signs and said yes to new beginnings. I always knew I would work with global brands, as my purpose was to create and build powerful ones. Did I know how? There is no concrete answer. I trusted the process that they would find me, and they did. Were there times when I was asked to do things that weren't within the scope of a brief I was given? Absolutely yes, and did I care? No. I saw it as an opportunity to make a difference. At one point I was the girl being asked to get the Thai takeaway delivery for a radio duo who went on to be number one in their market—collecting Thai from a delivery driver late at night was never in my brief to build them into a powerful brand. I chose to be that person because I knew I had to start at the bottom to make my way to the top. A simple "Yes, I can do that" to build loyalty, trust, and connection.

Never think something is beneath you; always look at the task and see if it has higher value because it will show you what you need to see. Through being the "runner," I became the storyteller and brand creator, setting them up with powerful media connections as they rose to the top of their game, becoming the highest-paid stars with that broadcast network. Who was trusted to create their first photo shoot for a brand campaign that appeared on every major transportation site in Australia when they landed their breakfast radio show? Me. I even brought along my six-week-old daughter because we shot it on a weekend. What was the purpose? It was my training ground to showcase my talents to a wider audience, just like that brand campaign did for them.

Remember, no matter what level you get to in business, someone will always ask you to get them a sandwich or a glass of wine. Just remind yourself there is always a mutual exchange of energy in life and a higher purpose; you just need to open your eyes to see it. We are born naked, and we die naked; in my eyes that makes us equal. It's the way you view the request that delivers the result!

CHAPTER THREE

The Power of Dreams

"When I see it, I believe it."

—Tory Archbold

I have always believed in the power of life and have experienced first hand the dreams many thought impossible translate into reality. A mindset and energy shift costs nothing. When you lead, you want to disrupt. Be courageous with your thinking and agile with your approach. By raising your vibration and taking a powerful step forward, knowing you can make a difference is what makes dreams come true. You will be remembered for the rules you break, not the ones you follow. I have always dreamed big and, despite the challenges I faced along the highway of life, I never doubted my ability to make those dreams reality. According to Lorimer Moseley, a professor of Clinical Neuroscience at the University of South Australia, I am "a highly proficient body listener." I put this down to the art of journaling and manifestation, trusting the process and following the signs, making me one of the 8 percent of the world's population who translates their dreams into reality. Let's use this chapter to bring the power of connection, but also the power of self-belief, intention, and manifestation to life so that you can become one of that 8 percent too.

So, what is a dream?

Dreams start when we are young and are often the result of rejection and failure. I personally like rejection and failure as they force us to look at options to place ourselves in a better situation or circumstance that empowers us to always look forward. We have the option to create what we want in our mindset, yet few make it reality as they hold onto fears and negative energies that abolish their ability to move forward. Building a healthy mindset through manifestation and journaling will set you apart from the crowd. I like how Eleanor Roosevelt phrased it: **"The future belongs to those who believe in the beauty of their dreams."** And yes, I am one of those who believe...and dream.

Take Libby Moore, transformational business coach and Oprah's former chief of staff, whom I connected with on a virtual coffee date and then interviewed on my *Powerful Stories* podcast. Her earliest dream recollection was that she wanted to be a cowboy. That was number one. Her second was to become an eighteen-wheeler truck driver. She wanted these two things because she wanted to travel and meet new people. Most importantly she wanted to work with others to deliver impact.

Libby is an extraordinary woman who backed her dreams and most importantly backed herself. She learnt the power of understanding that when a door wasn't opening the way she wanted, it was because something bigger was waiting.

She secured the role of Oprah's chief of staff through a portal of networking, connection, a mindset shift, and intention blessed with gratitude. After working as Jann Wenner's EA at *Rolling Stone* magazine, the doors she truly wanted to walk through to become a screenwriter were not opening. In fact, they seemed to be firmly shut. She said a prayer of intention and said, "OK, OK, clearly you don't want me writing for *Saturday Night Live* or Rosie O'Donnell because you know how badly I want it. I've been trying for eight and a half years, and nothing is happening. So, I am open. Whatever I am meant to do. Every Adam cell and molecule in my body, mind, and spirit is open to it. Show me what it is. Be clear and I will do it."

She released that intention into the universe, which meant she surrendered and was open to receiving whatever came next, which she refers to on my podcast as "a treasure hunt." When she stopped trying to force doors open great things started to unfold. Five weeks later an email came via a networking group, and she soon found herself by Oprah Winfrey's side, meeting and connecting with incredible people like Nelson Mandela and Dr. Maya Angelou. Here was her greatest dream—connect with others to create and deliver impact while learning from a wildly funny, intelligent, kind, generous, intuitive, wise woman. In Libby's words, to be by someone's side like that for over a decade was "the greatest gift."

Remember the movie *Sliding Doors*? It's iconic because it was about choice, a moment in time when the sliding door indicates you recognize change is coming and are about to step from a crossroad along a new highway of life to experience new beginnings, new opportunities, and new connections.

The dream meaning of sliding doors symbolizes effortless change, and those changes may be related to yourself, your work, your environment, or other people's ideas. If you dream of going through a sliding door, it reflects that the changes will make your life more comfortable. For several years before I shut the doors to my agency, my nightly dreams were a silent nudge that a crossroads and a new path were coming. I started to map out what this may look like in a journal, and I kept coming back to the same thought process—trust the timing of when it's meant to happen as the opportunity will present itself.

I believed I could start again and knew the next business journey would be more powerful than the last, so I tested my thought process, in effect my manifestation that wanted to be translated into reality. I started dropping into conversations that I was ready for new beginnings and what that would look like, and my narrative was simple and laced with intent—I wanted to empower others through the life lessons I had learnt, maybe write a book and shine a light for others through sharing the power of my story.

Radio silence. Not one person supported this idea and believed I should shut a perfectly good business to start another one. They shut me down, again...and again. As I was listening to the shutdown, I quickly recognized these people were not my tribe if they were unwilling to watch me back myself and embrace new beginnings. I knew the signs my intuition was trying to tell me something bigger and better was unfolding and it ticked my go-to signposts. So, while everyone else didn't think I was on the right track, I knew deep inside I was. I was having another "aha" moment and this time I was not afraid to leave the "nonbelievers" behind. You see, self-belief is my superpower.

This is my go-to checklist for when to follow the signs of life and how to know you are on track for transformation. Most importantly these signposts mean you are meant to trust the process and allow it to evolve to reveal the miracles coming your way. If you are mentally ticking these signs off as you read, you will know you are on the right track.

1. Your thoughts get pulled in a certain direction.

2. You feel happy and excited about an impulsive decision.

3. You feel uneasy about certain situations.

4. You have recurring dreams.

5. You are presented with the same choices.

6. You feel ready and engaged with your idea to move powerfully forward.

By following the signs, my thoughts and dreams kept nudging me day in and out and, although the pathway forward was still unclear, I could see my choices were different and new beginnings were on the way. Out of the blue we received a referral to launch Drew Barrymore's Flower Beauty in Australia. Trusting my gut instinct, it was an instant yes. I had a feeling this partnership would be life-changing and was willing to trust the process and follow the signs as the butterflies of change started fluttering again in the pit of my stomach, which meant my intuition was telling me to sit up and listen. Drew's most famous tattoo is of a butterfly representing faith, transformation, and freedom, and whenever I am faced with transformation they magically start appearing in my everyday life. When we first met, she gave the world's biggest hug and during our time together she spoke passionately about women, empowering them not to be invisible and sharing the power of their stories by stepping up and stepping forward. The synchronicities of life were at play and the signposts I was meant to follow became a reality for my next power move.

My daughter had never asked to have a photo with a celebrity I partnered with until she said, "Mum, I want to meet Drew Barrymore." Throughout my PR career I'd never had my photo with a celebrity because I believed my clients were, should, and always would be the star! Perhaps that's one of the reasons I owned sixty little black dresses—to blend into the background of everything I was engaged in creating.

My daughter insisted she skip school and I gave in. "Mum, Mum, can I come along to your event and let's have this photo with Drew?"

Drew said, "Tory, Tory, come in the photo."

As soon as a photographer clicked the camera at that event at Icebergs, an iconic venue every global celebrity wants to visit when they come to Sydney, my intuition said, "You're done. This part of your career is over. You are ready to step into the next more powerful part of your life journey that will be of service to others." That gut instinct I always trusted told me to step forward. I listened to my intuition at that moment, and it said, "I'm going to pass the baton. I've worked with so many incredible brands. It's time to translate myself into my own brand and show other people that if you share your story and own it, you will own your power and it will open the doors of opportunity in new and exciting ways."

That's how Powerful Steps was born, and I thank my daughter for that moment with Drew. It was about sharing what was going on behind the scenes of creating and building a global business—what was *really* going on behind closed doors in my personal life, which I'd never spoken about. I had kept the judgment, shame, and guilt to myself like an ongoing hangover from years of people-pleasing and hidden trauma. Suddenly, when I allowed myself to be fully me (authentic) and stepped out of the shadows and into the light, people finally said, "Oh, she's normal. Oh, this is what actually happened to her." They began to see me as human rather than the "PR powerhouse" I was known as. Sharing our humanity is powerful. When you have human connection you can take people on a journey, it's like a product or a service, and they want to stay on that journey with you if it's anchored to your truth.

Self-Care Is Non-negotiable

If you want to bring the power of your dreams to life, self-care is essential. How can you hear the whispers of life if you don't have a still mind? Many years ago, I was at a health retreat in Thailand and was burnt out. I had adrenal fatigue and chronic fatigue, and this Buddhist monk sat me down and he said, "You need to learn how to meditate."

And I said, "I'm too busy to meditate."

And he said, "No one is ever too busy." He taught me to always create space for myself in the morning, a space that allows me to tap into my intuition and most importantly a space that sets me up for success.

I remember questioning and pressuring him with, "How am I going to do that? I've got a global business. I've got a young daughter. I'm a single mom. I've got stuff going on."

He was not buying into my excuses and simply said, "Who do you have a shower with every day?"

I said, "Myself."

He replied, "That's where you're going to meditate."

The power of what he taught me has delivered my greatest breakthrough moments, but the catch is this: You need to slow yourself down so that you can listen to your inner voice from within. Start saying no to what does not set your heart on fire to create space for what does. If you're ready and willing to create the space needed to level up, this morning shower ritual will start shifting your energy and vibration so that you start attracting what you deserve, aligning you with your destiny. I am living proof this strategy works.

Every morning in the shower, I get some lavender oil. I put three drops on my decolletage. I inhale and exhale three times. Then, guess what I do? I listen. I listen to what I'm meant to be doing. Some of the best creative ideas, some of the best business ideas, and some of the best project connections have come from my morning shower ritual. When you focus on this morning ritual, tapping into your intuition because you've made the time to stop and listen to yourself and what your intuition will tell you, you start your day in the most powerful way because you are ready to follow the signs, and the signposts you are being shown will be powerful. It gives you the gift of trusting your intuition and knowing what doors are meant for you and what doors are meant for another. You no longer feel bitter and twisted that you didn't "win" that project or promotion. You simply know it is not meant for you and a bigger and better opportunity is waiting around the corner, ready to propel you forward.

I use the same shower ritual in the evening to end my day with gratitude. "Thank you for bringing this person into my life." "Thank you for that project opportunity." "Thank you for that connection." Honestly, I have never looked back, and the future has never looked brighter because I know this daily ritual delivers positive energy shifts and helps remove negative energy blocks.

Be sure to download your Morning Shower Ritual video training and guide from me in your digital bonuses at selfbeliefisyoursuperpower.com/bonus.

By claiming the power of our dreams, we can step into alignment with our destiny.

It doesn't matter the size of the step you take toward these dreams; what truly matters is that you made the conscious decision to move forward and shift the energy in your favor. If you take the approach to never look backward, and always look forward, these shifts will gain powerful momentum and you will become a magnet for miracles.

Let's revisit the story of my daughter. She said she wanted to sing. She had no formal voice training, and it was considered a risky move to start from scratch in a subject she had no experience in at a critical time in her final years of school. I've always encouraged her to trust her gut instinct, follow her dreams, and forget what others think as judgment prevents her from reaching her true potential. It's what you think and believe that counts along with a good dose of self-care and a happy heart. My attitude has always been $%#@! the naysayers—you can do anything you want in this lifetime; people can give an opinion and pass judgment but are they truly qualified to determine the outcome? Nine out of ten times the answer is no. You are the leader of your own destiny and that is what counts when you choose to step into your power.

When I won full custody of my daughter in 2017, and a restraining order was granted after twelve years of untold hell, I asked her how she wanted to celebrate, and we went on that roadtrip to see Celine Dion in Las Vegas. I believe through the power of music and that experience she stepped into her own power zone, leaving behind the trauma she had been through, so she only visualized and focused on her future and the outcome she desired. In her final year exam, she sang her favorite Celine Dion song in French from that concert; she mastered a new language to sing and was offered a music scholarship at a prestigious college. Did her school celebrate her talent? No, they did not—she got knocked back for every music award she was nominated for because she did not fit their "mould." Did the outside world recognize her gift? Yes, it did.

The moral of the story is:

◊ If you have a dream, don't be afraid to make it happen.

◊ Don't be afraid to place what you want at the top of your priority list.

◊ Never forget that it's the powerful steps we take in business and life that create the space for us to claim our crown and thrive.

◊ $%#@! the naysayers—they will be in your life for a hot minute—you're living your life...for life!

Catherine Bowyer is in her fifties and radiates happiness. She's the kind of woman who walks into a room and you just want to get to know her. Like every woman, no matter where they are located or what type of life they lead, she arrived at a crossroads. Catherine and I connected because she was ready to birth an up-leveled version of herself and I introduced her to the shower ritual in our Business Attraction Program. She already had a strong morning practice, yet this ritual took all of that to the next level and was a real game-changer. When she has her morning shower and places the lavender drops on her decolletage, she receives instant downloads—in her own words, "It's as though the lavender opens the gateway to my inner guide/intuition/spirit."

She asks a general question of "What do I need to know today?" or a more specific question about something that she would like an answer to or help with. Key outcomes that have shifted her mindset since doing this ritual are:

1. **Clarity of Thought**—Receiving clear messages that provide guidance and direction.

2. **Creativity**—By freeing her mind, amazing ideas flow in.

3. **Self-Belief**—The clear messages she now receives provide reassurance about what she's doing and where she's heading.

When Catherine receives a download, she gifts it with gratitude then sets her intention for the day. In her words: "I feel calm, relaxed, and start my day with ease and grace and a heart filled with happiness and love. I also think my water usage has gone up since doing this ritual as I tend to spend more time in the shower listening to the guidance!" By simply sharing what I was taught, Catherine can now share the power of what she has learnt with others too.

Through translating dreams into reality, you will come across life lessons. One of the earliest lessons in business I was given was to show compassion. I was asked to promote a high-profile comedy star and loved who she was and what she stood for. It was an incredible career moment when we secured a prestigious front-cover story with a major media outlet to celebrate a deal she had secured. A stylist, hair and makeup were booked, we briefed the client on the story and outcome, and everyone was excited until two weeks later when I received a call from the editor saying they were no longer running the story as a front cover as the talent was deemed "too ugly" to sell copies of the magazine. I was speechless—shouldn't a story run on the merit of the talent and how did "looks" play a part in what everyone knew to be a highly talented and inspirational woman of one of the country's top-rated shows? I rang my client to share the news and I was told that I needed to "break" the news to this woman whom I truly admired. Do I tell the truth or skirt around the truth? I chose to skirt around the truth because I believed no woman should be told they are too ugly to star in the story of their life. I told her it was my fault the story was pulled and, yes, she fired me as her publicist. Sometimes you must show compassion to keep others' dreams alive. I never saw her on another magazine cover, but I did see her bank millions because she was a highly talented woman who understood the power of her dreams.

THE POWER OF DREAMS

Not everyone will want to celebrate with you when you make a dream reality. Be OK with that. When you trust the process and embrace life lessons you are given, you will understand they came your way for a reason—to level up, to switch on your A game, or to switch your thinking. I know the bigger the challenge, the greater the opportunity because bigger things are meant to show up and become part of our life force so we can lead others. Be prepared to back your dream and yourself so you're ready to claim your crown.

Leaning Into Your Life Force Will Empower You

You can lean into your life force in seven ways. You can practice these mantras daily, or use the go-forward method of taking small steps that will one day become more powerful steps because you have shifted your mindset and energy to a higher vibration—the type of vibrational energy people notice when you walk into the room, causing others to want to be around you and get to know you and what you have to offer:

1. Practice acceptance.

2. Practice awareness.

3. Let go of limiting beliefs.

4. Allow yourself to be happy.

5. See thoughts and words as actions.

6. Overcome your feeling of separateness.

7. Feel the energy, name the emotions, and celebrate milestones.

When our life force is in short supply, we will feel ungrounded, lethargic, and depressed and struggle to move through life. Integrating conscious intention empowers us to move into higher states of mental and emotional energy that can revitalize our physical and subtle bodies. Now imagine if you tap into your life force, align your every move with your value set and trust your gut instinct—I would say that's a powerful toolkit. And guess what? That toolkit is free. It belongs to you.

Take Powerful Steps and Work in Life's Flow

We all operate at a level, sometimes in life, where we think, "You know, I really want that opportunity, but why aren't I attracting it?" or "Why hasn't it come to me?" There's always a simple solution. When you're in life's flow, you understand that what's coming for you and what's meant for you will naturally evolve and find its way to you. What's meant for someone else will always do the same for them in return. When you miss out on an opportunity, don't go, "That was mine; I needed that. Why didn't I get it?" Tap yourself on the shoulder and say, "Thank you for the opportunity, and whoever's meant to have it, may they be blessed with good fortune and abundance because I know something bigger and better will come my way." And...wait patiently!

There is no exact timeframe in life; it's not like someone can give you a magic bullet to attract what you want—if this existed, someone somewhere would be a trillionaire. This philosophy to trust life's flow truly does work because I have learnt the hard way to believe in that process. It won't be easy, but you probably know that already!

The best example I can give is that a few years ago I took a step back from running my agency to create the space to focus on my daughter and bring my life into alignment. During this timeframe, I became invisible to many people, and I was happy with that until one day I was at an event and realized I was becoming invisible and irrelevant within my industry. I was no longer the leader or disrupter as I had handed that over to my team. That feeling was like a kick in the ass, that prod you need to feel when you know you need to accept it's time for new beginnings and step into your power *again*.

So, what did I do? I trusted the power of the universe and the process of what these new beginnings might look like by following the signs shown to me each day during my morning shower ritual. My gut instinct told me something bigger was at play. I was committed to this ritual and given the powerful steps through morning downloads that I needed to take to show my relevance, who I needed to connect with, and most importantly, who I needed by my side to prepare for the changes ahead.

Within six weeks of feeling irrelevant, I was suddenly highly empowered and relevant again. This was no coincidence. It was a miracle at play—a miracle I had actively participated in. In a short time frame, I shifted my life force energy to win Victoria's Secret, a billion-dollar lingerie brand and at the time the number one lingerie brand in the world, Steve Madden, the billion-dollar shoe man, and Drew Barrymore, one of America's most successful movie stars and an entrepreneur to launch Flower Beauty in Australia as clients.

The gift was this—I waited, trusted the process, and was given the three biggest brands in America. It was because **what was coming for me was meant for me, and what was coming for someone else was meant for them.** If you can use that affirmation and not get frustrated when things don't go well, you do not feel judged, irrelevant, or lose yourself to fear. Instead, you can live in flow and alignment, which means you can 100 percent step into your power zone and meet your destiny.

Finding your life flow can be tough. For a decade, a limited number of people knew of a challenging and traumatic time I had with my ex and at times it felt terrifying. After a decade of dealing with this abusive situation, there was no resolution in sight, and I needed to crack a solution. To help navigate a positive way forward I hired a mentor from Chicago, an ex-lawyer from a Fortune 100 company who had experienced burnout and turned her life around. She was positive and powerful and made me accountable to the end game, which I needed. When we began working together, I thought I would never see the light at the end of the tunnel. I was wearing two masks and finding it hard to keep my head above water in business and life.

Some time had passed, and she said, "Tory, you're 75 percent there."

And I said, "But when am I going to be 100 percent through the tunnel?"

Right? It's the biggest question in life. And she said, "The lessons are going to keep coming to you until you learn them. Only when you show the universe that you've learnt them, it'll be 80 percent. It'll be 90 percent. It will be 100 percent. Then you'll have that breakthrough." The key to trusting this process is to follow signs and never give up on those big thoughts and dreams because they eventually become a reality. This mentor helped me claim my keys to freedom. I hit rock bottom and then received wings to fly.

We're all born with the right to step into our power zone. Our power zone can be defined as a feeling of ultimate self-power and strength because we live each moment in alignment with our truth and destiny. It's a zone that best reflects our life force because we have mastered the art of surrendering to receive the right outcome for that moment—we recognize this moment can be a challenge or a possibility and we are not fussed either way, as we know it's for our highest and greatest good. On the professional front and on the personal front, we're all unique and have the right to live in that zone. What's not to love about those facts? The fact is we need to start somewhere to map out our life plan before mother nature taps us on the back and says it's time to go. Some of the biggest regrets people have before they pass are wishing they'd had the courage to live a life true to them, not the life others expected them to become—they were trapped in the box of expectations and weren't prepared to jump. Others wished they had the courage to express their feelings more clearly and had taken a different path in life when they were at a crossroads.

If you're like me and want to live and die without regrets at a high vibrational level and in your power zone, invest in a personal vision statement. A personal vision statement is a statement that describes your values, strengths, and goals and will become your go-to everyday mantra.

It can be focused on life or professional goals (like a bucket list of places to travel) and is intended to orient you toward long-term dreams and internal fulfillment. Having a clear vision takes you places and sets you up for success. I recommend tapping into the power of this statement daily in your morning showing ritual as the more you lean into the power of what you want the more likely it is to become your reality. When you make an effort to shift your energy and thoughts forward daily you can embrace life to its highest, fullest potential and see greater opportunities present themselves. Say yes to opportunities rather than no or "maybe next time" as when your intent and vision statement is clear your purpose lights up the world around you and the opportunities that come for you will be more in alignment with who you are and what you want to become in this lifetime.

Create a vision board in your home, office, or on Pinterest that you can refer to, and tap into the power of the signposts along the highway of life that will become your reality. During this process, you may discover that perhaps you were meant to walk a different path than you are currently on, and that's OK. When you become agile in your thinking, you will see the challenges you need to learn before the doors open for you to walk through and claim your crown.

CHAPTER FOUR

How to Feed Your Soul and Create Miracles

"There is not one single person in the world you need more than yourself. When you celebrate and lean into the power of who you are, watch how your life changes. That simple mindset shift is the creator of miracles."

—Tory Archbold

I have always kept a journal. In fact, you will find hundreds of them in our home along with social media platforms I have created of quotes and affirmations that inspire me. Here are three of my favorites:

The master sees things on the way, not in the way.

Passion changes everything.

Dreams don't work unless you do.

I started leaning into the power of journaling in my twenties. I had returned from London and started a job I loved leading a team in promotions in Sydney. I was only there for a heartbeat because a member of my family knew a top media recruiter and she thought I would be better placed in another role in media on a little-known PAY TV channel. I was given the title of promotions manager and a salary decrease of $20,000, as they had both talked me into this role being a great career move when I knew in the pit of my stomach it wasn't—I couldn't even afford my rent. I simply people-pleased and accepted the box they wanted to place me in, ignoring my gut instinct. Arriving at an open-plan office on the first day of this role I was told to share a desk with my assistant, which was stacked high above the computer with manila folders collecting dust, which we were both expected to share (no storage; folders were all over the floors, under desks—complete shambles and a reflection of the marketing team of that era). I had come from a glass office in the promotional agency leading an awesome, results-driven team and had decided to move against my intuition, so I had to suck it up. I lasted less than three months and never had a desk to call my own. They fired me for not being able to communicate with talent, not being able to send a courier, and something else I can't recall. Communicating and connecting with others is one of my business superpowers and my manager hated that. I always wanted to create and do more and she always wanted to push back and find excuses for not leveling up or finding me a desk. It was never going to work.

Being fired delivered a gift of three months' pay. I booked a trip to Bali that same day I was fired, having been given the opportunity to deep dive, manifest, and journal about what I truly wanted in my career. It was not to be boxed; it was to be valued. It was to partner with the best of the best who saw my talent as an asset. To this day I still have that yellow Balinese journal I wrote these aspirations and vision statements in and feel almighty blessed they came true. And you know another fun fact—don't fear losing your job; everyone will get fired at least once in their lifetime. It's to level you up to the next life vibration and attract the right tribe and vibe you deserve. That channel no longer exists and I'm happy to say I do! Thank you, universe—lesson learnt, always trust your gut instinct.

Tapping into powerful affirmations, manifestation, and journaling will help you clarify thoughts, feelings, and your life direction. Investing time to journal regularly allows you to track life patterns to discover what truly sets your heart on fire and most importantly what you need to let go of to create space for new beginnings and opportunities. Through journaling, you can be brutally honest with yourself and learn about your true inner power, purpose, and intent without sharing a single word with another person. The more you take the time to write down your thoughts, feelings, and ambitions the clearer the pathway becomes and the easier it is to break the patterns that are holding you back. Through this process you will be 100 percent shifting your energy forward through the power of your words, which I always find exciting!

There are no rules about what you can write about—journaling is about you and when you understand the power of *you* your pathway becomes clearer. This process has empowered me to overcome some of the biggest obstacles in my life, to understand the patterns that led me to the same life lessons on repeat, and most importantly, it has taught me the power of who I am and what I am capable of when I don't buy into what others think. I have learnt that this is their story projection, and this is mine. We cannot rewrite history—yesterday is done and dusted, and tomorrow will always wait for us to embrace it. Be clear on what you want because you will attract what you deserve. The clearer your thought process, the more likely it is to come to life if you attach the desire with a breakdown of steps you will take to make it happen. That's a *big* shift of energy you are asking the universe to move forward with so look at what you have written often. Tick off what has happened and add a gratitude page to say thank you and always add another powerful manifestation to the list because, we are on planet earth to evolve and grow. What I have learnt is that it is never too late to start again.

Remember, you're likely to attract some speed humps along the highway of life. Write about them and own them because the thing about speed humps is when you own them, you're allowed to ride over them because there is always another journey and way forward on the other side. When you don't learn the "life lesson," speed humps will keep appearing, which can be frustrating. My advice is to look at yourself in the mirror, own your mistake or part in the "story," and resolve it internally or externally so you keep moving your story forward. A speed hump–free highway is the ultimate life journey—some might call it nirvana.

You can start journaling and manifesting your future by:

1. **Creating space in your day, which is about you.** It can be as little as five, ten, or twenty minutes; it doesn't matter. What matters is that you take time for yourself daily.

2. **Writing the first thing that comes into your mind.** It's usually a dream or a challenge, but it may vary. It could also be a question or an idea.

3. **Breaking down your feelings around what you write down.** This is the *how* and/or *why* and your proposed next step to prep forward. This is called conscious creation. We are what we think and believe. The more we write, say, and live in alignment with our dream, the more it becomes a reality.

4. **Commit daily.** Rinse and repeat the process, making it a practice you do every day.

5. **Take the time to read over what you have written.** The more you believe in the dream, the more likely you are to make the powerful steps to take them forward into reality.

Think *Big* by Goal Setting

Think back to when you were a student. I was an average student with 50 to 60 percent marks and the occasional failure. The talker and the disruptor—the girl on the sidelines nobody believed or invested in. The one they wanted to marry off to have three kids and a nice family home. I surprised everyone in my graduating year because I got 87.75. I always remember that number because I even blew myself away. No one thought I could do it, and I didn't put that much effort into it. When I received the results I thought, "Wow, I didn't put that much effort into that. Imagine if I put effort into my life, what would happen, what I could create." And that's the power of how I learnt to think *big* through a simple mindset switch, which became my superpower and is called self-belief.

When you have nothing to lose, you have everything to gain. I started with zero money in the bank. I had no connections. I was not degree educated. I built a global business. I've been involved in multi-million-dollar, hundred-million-dollar M&A deals for other people, and the crazy part of my story is I was their spokesperson and their mouthpiece as they often did not know how to articulate their product, service, or wins. This is my advice—step into your power, stay in your lane, and compare yourself to no one. Lean into the possibilities of what you can do and don't worry about making mistakes because you will make them. In fact, you will make a *lot* of them. Consider them life lessons that empower you to step up and into the person you are meant to be—not the expectations of a role someone else wants you to play.

The Five Powerful Steps to *Think Big*

1. **Stick to Your Values.** They become a magnet superpower and open you up to opportunities in alignment with your truth.

2. **Marinate in Sh*t Rule.** A Buddhist monk in northern Thailand once told me that I could pretend my problem was a pile of shit—literally. Did I want to step into and smell that pile of shit and marinate in it? Well, clearly, *no!* These are the three choices he gave me to view my problem—you can marinate in it for forty-five years, forty-five minutes, or forty-five seconds. The choice is yours and yours only. If you choose forty-five years, that's half your life—gone. It took me a few years to go from forty-five minutes to forty-five seconds and now this forty-five-second rule helps me live life with flow and ease.

3. **Connecting with People Is Your Most Powerful Tool.** It shows you are open and available to opportunities.

4. **Go on Coffee Dates.** Commit to charging your energy with others and follow my non-negotiable formula for building a successful business and life with a commitment to three coffee dates a week.

5. **Put Yourself First.** If you're not happy, the people around you will not be happy. Build this affirmation into your daily ritual "a happy heart is a magnet for miracles." It truly does work to shift your mindset and energy, which is your super attractor to connect with the right people in the right Divine timeframe.

Translate Your Dream into Reality

Transformations are never easy, which is why so many people give up on their dreams. The most common reason people do not move forward is fear of the unknown. They lose the belief that it is possible and become distracted by other aspects of their life. I never questioned my self-belief since graduating high school because I framed my mindset with, "I can do this" and "I will do this." It was simply a matter of being clear on what I wanted to create and aligning my energies to deliver the result. That's not to say that times weren't tough, they 100 percent were, and I have been one of those women who has sold her clothes to place food on the table at various stages of my career. Leaning into tough times strengthened my belief that comebacks were better than setbacks. Those experiences delivered life lessons that allowed me to become humble, compassionate, and empathetic to others because I had learnt experience. If you're not willing to step outside of your comfort zone to operate in your power zone, then making your dream a reality is not a life option and that's OK too. If you are ready to step up—invest time in doing the inner work, learn the hard way, and unleash your brilliance. You've got this.

Entrepreneur, TV personality, and wellness warrior Sally Obermeder has been my friend for two decades and we click because we both believe in the motto "never give up." When we are faced with a challenge we always ask, "How can we conquer it?" When people say no, we ask, "How can we make them say yes?" In 2011 when my agency partnered with Zara to launch in the Australian market with a dynamic brand communication strategy, they said no to the media having the opportunity to experience the brand before the official launch date. I had been lucky enough to understand their global footprint and story experiences through my travels around the world and when briefing media on the launch spoke with such passion about Paris, Rome, and Dubai, they wanted to experience that same passion I had for the brand, and they wanted to be first to share it with others on their media platform. At the time Sally worked for a TV network with the most-watched current affairs news platform in the country—she reached out and asked if it was a possibility and I explained it wasn't. She asked, "What if we could make this happen?" Great question because I wanted to make this happen too as my intuition told me this would be a launch like no other in our country. So, we hatched a plan and were bold and courageous while respecting the boundaries given to my agency as a representative partner of the brand.

We workshopped "what if" scenarios and decided the best one would be to trust our instinct and intuition that this would deliver the most incredible insight for the Australian customer who was not aware of the brand (we are talking pre-online shopping times here). The best way to bring the brand experience to life would be to show others how it was created, who was behind it, and how it would be a brand they could have an ongoing connection with simply because they could see it would give them a fast-fashion solution for their wardrobe needs at affordable pricing. When my client said no, we said yes and Sally hopped on a plane to Spain as the scenario we had played out was, "What if I just showed up in Spain from a country twenty-four hours away? Would they turn me away?" I think Inditex, Zara's parent company, probably thought "How are these bold and brave Aussies who are so in love with our brand crazy enough to fly halfway around the world at their own expense?" Our answer was simply, "Because we love what we do and want to make a difference."

In a world first, they granted access to the never-seen-before behind-the-scenes business operations, and I remember when Sally showed me some of the footage before it aired. I watched in awe of the passion of the people riding bikes around in the warehouse, ensuring that this business ticked with passion and purpose. When Zara launched in Australia, teamwork delivered an experience beyond anyone's imagination. A total of 22,000 people queued up to walk through the doors on day one and one million dollars in sales was generated. These people had flown in from around Australia, many of them turning up because of that one segment we had created, and they had watched simply because we dared to dream *big*, and we believed in the brand and our purpose. This launch is often quoted as the "biggest launch in retail history" and is one of the most Googled case studies on successful retail brand launches in the world.

Zara, I simply salute you and your courageous team—you dreamed *big* and became the number one retail brand in the world from a small village in Spain to deliver impact for billions who have had the privilege of experiencing your stores. You never once wavered on that dream or your values. The lesson is always to partner with others who are your energetic match by aligning partnerships with values. We all worked with passion, integrity, and delivery, which are my three foundational values in life and business—and for the brand that was a 100 percent energy match.

When you dream *big* you also need to have an achievable goal set so you can claim that dream with confidence—just like Sally and I did all those years ago. Goal setting is a powerful life tool as it allows you to think about your future, motivates you to step into change, and ultimately translates your future vision into reality. Many people will advise you to work out a road map and tick a box. Sometimes ticking boxes does not create a successful business—it creates a system and if the business has no heart, soul, or ability to be agile the customer journey fails. I've enjoyed two successful businesses and never had a plan for either when they were created. I had myself and the belief I could make an impact through the power of connection and communication. I had an idea for each business, which I continuously journaled and intently manifested with powerful thoughts of how it would look like, who I would like to partner with, who would be in my team, what global impact I could deliver through following the signs as they appeared and trusting my intuition. Sounds crazy? It may be, but that's the truth.

If you are goal-setting, think about what is realistic for you. Every January after the new year, it is not realistic for me to lose three to five kilos before February. This is when I invest in family, friendships, travel, and recharge after a busy previous year. I am not going to say no to a glass of rose or French bubbles with friends or the opportunity to host a dinner party only to say, "Sorry, I can't eat or drink that." What I can do is make realistic self-care goals that I know are possible to achieve. This year my goal was to have a facial every three weeks because I recognized I needed more downtime away from digital devices and being "available" as I was building a new business, which meant energy investment beyond a normal working week. Six months in, I was still committed to this goal as it was achievable. The benefits are real—100 percent nonnegotiable "me time," which is good for your mental health as you can recharge your body without distraction for ninety minutes. An added benefit? My skin looks better than ever.

The key to goal-setting is to set goals unique to you that excite, inspire, and grow you to the next level. Remember goal-setting can help you in any area of your life, from achieving financial freedom to adopting a healthy diet.

When you learn how to set goals in one area of your life, it becomes easier to set them in other areas. Below are some examples of goals you may wish to consider as they fall into the top most-wanted goals to attain in the world—yes, I always like to reach for the stars, and I trust you do too. I've listed seven because that is my favorite number and birth date!

1. Become an inspiration to others.

2. Master a difficult skill.

3. Become a thought leader in your industry.

4. Get promoted to an executive role in your company.

5. Learn how to become a millionaire.

6. Go on a trip around the world.

7. Travel to your dream country.

I met with Antonia Kidman over a memorable coffee date in Singapore many years ago and we spoke about goal-setting. I asked, "How are you doing?"

She said, "I'm ready for change. I think I'm going to go and do a law degree." She had six children between two countries at that point and was in her forties, and I asked why she wanted this sudden big life change.

When we spoke years later on my podcast she said, "I would say it doesn't matter what age you are, you gotta do it. Because this is the future. I want to work until I finish, until it's all over. There's no end date for me because I like it. I need to have purpose in my life."

Antonia created the space for herself to study and achieve the goal. She recognized she had a baby, a toddler, the kids, and all the rest of it but was structured. Her superpower is that she is incredibly disciplined. She translated her dream into reality by leaning into that strength and is now a lawyer specializing in family law, creating and delivering impact for others by helping them navigate their life journeys.

So, the key to making your dreams a reality is truly simple. Follow Antonia's lead and simply create the space, step up, and make it happen.

CHAPTER FIVE

Attract the Right Partners with a Powerful Personal Brand

*"If you want to build a standout professional
and personal brand, you need to advocate
not just for yourself, but advocate for others."*

—Tory Archbold

I am always asked what the logic is behind having a standout personal brand. Most importantly, what is a personal brand versus a business brand? How do you get the scripting, storytelling, and positioning right to connect with other like-minded people? My feelings on this are people will not connect with you unless they feel that you're in alignment with the values, intent, and purpose of your business and service. If you understand who you are, are clear on your intent and purpose, and most importantly, anchor your storytelling to your values, you will attract what you deserve. Sounds simple, but I'm going to dive deep and tell you how I have managed to build powerful global brands while building my brand brick by brick, laying that foundation, anchoring it to my values, intent, and purpose to attract what I deserve while serving others.

To elevate your life and attract what you deserve you need to do the inner work on brand you and it's what I consider nonnegotiable. When you hit a roadblock and feel that you are off-piste it comes back to that age-old saying—you can't attract the right people until you are right within yourself. It's a tough process but I know it's worth the pain. Creating the time to find balance in all parts of life so we are placed in a position to attract the miracles ready for us to receive is the first powerful step we can take. This means acknowledging and accepting who we face each day in the mirror—ourselves—and being happy with what we see and feel from the inside out.

Let's start this process by talking about personal branding. Your brand must showcase who you authentically are. What do you see in the mirror? Do you understand who you are, your actual life story? Have you accepted what that story is? Are you in alignment with your truth? While you're reading this, take a moment to reflect and give a silent nod of yes or no because most people around the world do not know who they are, let alone the power they can unleash within them to achieve great things because they fear claiming their crown by owning the truth of their story, their unique digital footprint, and the gifts they were given at birth.

Let me explain my situation and story to give you some perspective. For many years, while working in my own business, I had twenty-two staff, two personal assistants—one for business and one to help me navigate being a single mama bear of one—that empowered me to partner with the most incredible brands, celebrities, and influencers around the world. The non-glossy reality was I was wearing two masks and not owning my truth because I was afraid people would judge me if I told them what happened behind closed doors when I got home. I felt that if I was truthful about what was truly happening, all the trauma, drama, stalking, and harassment I went through with my ex, others would judge me.

It wasn't until I aligned with my truth after a near-death "mirror" experience in 2013 that I stood in my power by creating space for new beginnings and in return received the keys to freedom. I learnt that the discovery of choice does not involve conditions. We all must face reality at some stage of life or the situation we are in and make a choice—and mine was not marinating in an awfully smelly shit for another forty-five years with the wrong people by my side. When I woke up in the ICU, I realized I was surrounded by takers, users and people in my immediate circle who did not have my best interests at heart. Some of the first questions asked by this circle were not, "Are you OK and how can we help you?" it was, "If you can't work, who will pay for the costs to look after your daughter because we can't?" and my favorite: "Can you give me eight thousand dollars to pay off my credit card bill as I helped save your life?" I was even given a box of battered Cadbury chocolates, which would apparently make me "feel better" even though the last thing you want to do when you lose eight kilos in five days while fighting septicaemia is eat a Cadbury chocolate as a first or supplementary meal. It's not that I was ungrateful for them showing up, I was truly grateful; it showed me it was time to move forward in a positive, more enlightened way with a tribe that aligned with what I wanted to move forward with versus what I wanted to leave behind. Just as we have various milestones in our modern education system, we also have them in our spiritual journey when we come out the other side of a traumatic experience, and mine was clarity. Clarity to gently say goodbye to those relationships that had taught me some of my greatest life lessons and be open to receive the miracles of better energy, people and flow. To be with people who believed in a mutual exchange of energy.

As I am typing this, I realize from 2013 to 2017, a lot happened that enabled me to step into my power and own my story and that process has a name—transformation, which is an act or process of changing completely. How can you step up and into your power and attract the right opportunities if you have something holding you back? You can't and it's impossible as you will never find your "happy place" if you are not addressing the energy block inside of you and loving what is looking back at you as you face the mirror each day. You can release an energy block to move forward with your life in four ways:

1. Acknowledge your feelings.

2. Work through trauma.

3. Make intentional moves.

4. Practice stillness.

You can raise your vibrational energy through breathwork, which I highly recommend. Rhythmic deep breathing is a proven way to realign your vibrational energy when you are faced with trauma; meditation, gratitude, generosity, diet, outdoor immersion, therapeutic touch, healing touch, and Reiki—I embraced it all to know myself from the inside out because my daily mantra was "a happy heart is a magnet for miracles," and I wanted that happy heart to embrace the next journey of life I knew was coming.

Early on, I did not attract the right "personal life" partners and I must take ownership of that. I did not know myself and felt I was not worthy as I was not practicing self-kindness or self-care. It was time to change that fact, as I was after that happy heart and that meant facing my past to clear the pathway for the future. I decided to remove the shackles of life holding me back to receive full custody of my daughter and a restraining order to remove the daily trauma we were subjected to and had kept hidden from the world through fear and shame. My best friend inspired me to take positive action when she said, "You have spent a decade in the family law court, spending hundreds of thousands of dollars, and your lawyer can't wrap this agreement up? If you can create and build powerful brands for everyone else, why can't you resolve this matter for the two of you so you can move on?" That was my lightbulb moment. Boom! I did not have the "right professional partner" representing us. My self-belief kicked in, I got rid of our long-term lawyer, and I represented myself for the next two years, tapping into our key learnings, the power of what we had been through. I knew that I could find a solution that was best for my daughter and protected us.

In 2017, we were granted the answer to our prayers by the Family Law Court of Australia, and other women asked me if I could represent them or help them navigate their traumatic cases. It's not my skill set but my advice to them was it can become your skill set if you dig deep enough within your soul and believe there is a solution, as anything is possible with self-belief. Believe you can and you will. Always take 100 percent ownership and responsibility for what you contributed to the situation, trust the process, and believe you can deliver the outcome. I found forgiveness for what we had been through as I learnt this part of our journey was what empowered me to sit back and go, "What next?" For me that next powerful move was sharing the truth of what was happening in my life behind closed doors. It took two more years to have the courage to step forward and do that. I no longer felt judged and instead felt empowered, as I had achieved what many people believed was impossible simply by owning what was not right in my life. It changed the narrative of my life story and I found that I attracted a higher vibrational type of person into my life from that point forward.

I decided to share the power of my story and partner with a media outlet I 100 percent trusted that had also been on a journey with me but didn't know what was happening behind the scenes. That media outlet was *Marie Claire* magazine, at the time the number one women's magazine in the world. I will always be grateful for Nikki Briger, the editor of that magazine, who dedicated an incredible journalist to write why my story was one of success and survival, but most importantly how I took powerful steps to learn those life lessons, to step up, evolve into me, the woman I am today, where I'm able and capable of doing things differently, to lead and disrupt the way women traditionally think and operate.

Where do you start? By taking a powerful step toward your future self and owning who you are.

We will dive deep into your special personal brand and show you how to showcase what you want to attract into your life and business by revealing who you truly are. Are you ready? It's a brave move. You must be courageous and willing to be fearless to take ownership of your story. This means finding your superpower and strength you might have to reveal the deep dark truth of what's happened, which can be incredibly painful and scary; journaling, a therapist, or a friend can help. This deep dive can be just for you or it can be to lead by example for others. When you reframe your thinking around your raw and real-life story, you realize you are not alone and someone else has gone down that same highway or had that same tough experience, arriving at the same crossroads as you, and they had a choice to make. If you share it, you've leveled up, taken ownership of the outcome, and can shine a light and be of service for others. You can put this into place with your personal experiences or your professional experiences. It's the same philosophy. If you need validation or endorsement, ask a friend just like I did.

Accepting your story allows you to stand in your power. You don't fear judgment or the loss of family and friends; you just know what you're doing is right because you are in tune with your intuition and are ready to embrace change. So, when I decided to launch Powerful Steps, I had to be truthful about what happened. Why was I closing my successful brand communication agency? Why was I, in my forties, starting another business from scratch? Well, the answer was simple. I was in my power: I was standing in my truth. I understood that I could say, "Hey, this is me." Many of you reading this book maybe have or are experiencing the same trauma, harassment, lifetime experiences, and challenges I have, but guess what? At that crossroads, I took the right road, chose the right one, and I ended up where I am today, shining a light for you. That is how I faced my fear by leveling up, which means I can carry a light wherever I go.

You start this process by understanding your brand. Focus on getting the scripting right—the scripting is anchoring yourself to your values. What are your values? Break them down. Mine have always been passion, integrity, and delivery. I love being around passionate people because of their actions, who they surround themselves with, the brands they represent, and the teams they lead. That is important to me. The second value is integrity. I don't want to be around assholes, but I also want to be aligned with brands and people who stand in their truth, speak their truth and are not afraid to put their hands up and say, "Hey, I don't want to do that. That's not in my remit because it's not an alignment with who I authentically am."

The last value that anchors me to my personal branding story is delivery. I know I'm only as good as the last podcast chat, the last Zoom call, the last mentoring session and the last person who has gone through one of my programs and experienced that transformational moment. Your positioning comes from anchoring yourself to three core values, anchoring yourself to your intent and purpose. People will 100 percent connect with you if they feel you align with their values, intent, and purpose. Your brand will always anchor and showcase what you want to attract into your life or business. Importantly, it will reveal who you truly are and who you are ready to serve.

Building a personal brand is also about building powerful connections and partnerships. When we talk about powerful connections, again, that aligns with who you are authentically, and that alignment is to your value set. It's not about smoke and mirrors. It's about being authentically you. When I was asked to share the power of my story on the *Leading Women* podcast it was alongside CEOs and award-winning business owners. My story was different as I backed myself from a young age when others graduated from university or enjoyed a cadetship in a Fortune 100 company. When asked about the power of my leadership journey my answer was simple. It began with rejection and that rejection propelled me into the woman I am today. I had decided in my morning shower ritual on the day we recorded the podcast that more women needed to hear the brutal, raw truth, which would remove their thought process from the polished CEO script most people follow when they are interviewed so that others could clearly "see" that rejection can become your secret weapon in business and life. It meant I had to share the raw, authentically "me" side in this chat and so I did, and it paid off. That episode became the most downloaded conversation across three series and the number one bank in Australia called me in for a meeting to celebrate.

Over the years I built a formidable reputation by committing to three coffee dates a week. Why did I do that? Because I wanted to align and connect with like-minded people. I wanted to share what I could offer them. And most importantly, I wanted to hear how I could help them and always viewed these coffee dates as a mutual exchange of energy. Connect with others weekly when you're building a personal brand or a business to anchor yourself and build that authentic, truthful global network by committing to human connection.

That connection could be someone you've worked with in a previous role, someone you've worked with in a new role or someone you have lunch with once a week. It could be anyone you would consider a part of your ultimate community. You've met them several times; it's time to catch up, it's time to exchange ideas, exchange different ways that you can leverage each other's relationships and networks so you can both step up and into your A game. Also, consider partnership. Always have a partnership in mind to grow your business and your brand. It is the most powerful tool in the world. And of course, it doesn't cost anything if you partner with the right people because, again, it's a mutual exchange of energy, which is building your brand, product, or service you represent.

Some of the best opportunities I have been given come from partnership dates when I traveled between Australia and the US. I would always tag on a couple of extra days in LA and have coffee dates with people because I never knew who I might meet or what I might learn. I had an agency that represented incredible brands. My aim was to partner with other like-minded agencies who had the same caliber of clients, and I wanted to see how we could collaborate, because when you have a mutual exchange of energy, but also databases and shared value, intent, and purpose, that's where the magic happens because you can quickly double, triple, quadruple your reach for minimum output. And when we talk about minimum output, it's simple—you don't have to put large advertising dollars behind a smart partnership campaign to create and deliver impact. When the energy exchange is right, a miracle will appear.

If you want to stretch yourself, connect outside of your comfort zone. When we talk about the stretch in life, whether we are a corporate warrior, an entrepreneur, starting a side hustle, re-entering the workforce, or we've been made redundant, outside of our comfort zone at times can feel incredibly overwhelming. Now I want you to think about it like this. Have a list of five people, put them on your manifestation board, and work out how to meet them. I'll give you an example.

One of my beautiful clients, a runner-up for the Telstra Woman of the Year Award, a prestigious award for women in leadership in Australia, said, "Tory, I had on my manifestation board that I was one day going to meet Oprah."

And I said, "Did you meet her?"

And she said, "Yes, I did."

I said, "How did you make that happen?"

And she said, "Every day for two years I sent an email to her team introducing myself, but also telling them how, if I met her, it would be a mutual exchange of energy, and this is what we could create together."

I said, "How did that go down? Two years is a long time." Well, when Oprah decided to come to Australia, one of her team members emailed her and said, "Hey, Erica, would you like to meet Oprah?"

Now that's dedication. That is twenty-four months of connecting and manifesting in the off-chance that Oprah or someone on her team would receive, acknowledge, and advance that request to a meeting. So, dreams do come true. Think big, like Erica. I have Oprah on my manifestation board as well, and I truly hope that one day we get to have a coffee date. I also have Michelle Obama, Sharon Stone, and Jay Shetty—a mix including the most amazing people you probably have never heard of, but I know are creating global impact. They're on that list because I know they're outside of my comfort zone and some crazy opportunity will occur in my life where our paths cross and we're going to create magic together. So never lose the belief that those outside your comfort zone can cross your path as dreams come true when you believe in the magic of miracles.

If you want to build a standout professional brand, you need to advocate for yourself and others. The best way to do this is LinkedIn, as it has billions of people logging on every day, creating content, liking, engaging, and scourging for information. Your LinkedIn bio needs to be powerful as it drives your personal brand SEO on Google's algorithms. Those first three sentences are the standout about who you are, your intent and purpose, and most importantly, what you're capable of delivering. This also includes investing in having a photo at a brand shoot that showcases your true self and energy field for your profile shot or ad banner. Do not put up a photo with dead eyes because someone's said, "Hey, I just want to take your photo and we're going to put that up as a corporate shot," and it's looking bland, or "Hey, I really love this photo of me at a cocktail party, but I'm just going to cut the other person out and possibly no one's going to see that arm wrapped around me and that will be my LinkedIn profile."

I'm talking about a standout "look at me, this is me in my power-loving life" photo that shows the authentic, true you, which means that you have the right energy, look, feel, and representation of your brand to attract the right people and opportunities. In your LinkedIn bio, you also want to reveal something about yourself that is not just professional and all the amazing things you've achieved—something that most people don't know about you. So, for instance, when I was redoing my LinkedIn profile a few years ago, I worked with a copywriter who said, "Tory, what's something that not many people know about you being in your forties?"

And I said, "I got married at forty-six."

And she said, "And because of your success and survival story, this is obviously your second marriage."

And I said, "Guess what? I did not marry the father of my daughter."

She said, "Get out of town. Everyone thinks that you did."

I said, "No, I absolutely did not."

I was a single mom in the purest sense. So, we wrote in my LinkedIn profile at the time not only did Drew Barrymore empower me to end my PR career, but hey, I was a bride in my forties. Guess what happened? Other women, entrepreneurs, hardworking leaders in corporate, who, like me, for so many years were focused on the career climb and not so much on their personal life, started reaching out to say, "Hey Tory, I read your LinkedIn bio and oh my gosh, how did you find love in your forties?"

So, guess what? That fun fact about you is a conversation starter. Think about that one thing that you might be a little, "Oh, is it too cringy to put on my LinkedIn profile? Is this too cringy to tell people?" And sit with it, marinate it in, and just go, "Fuck it," and put it on there—because let me tell you, it helps build your brand 100 percent. When you share your challenges and let people see your raw side as I did—success and survival, but also guess what, hey, I was married in my forties—rather than looking you up and down, people will look up to you. So, switch up your LinkedIn profile and update it every three months because life changes and so do you—for the better if you are reading this book!

Please remember—don't be like everyone else and leave a flattering photo from years ago. Make sure you have that amazing magnetic image of you attracting what you deserve as a reflection of who you are right now. If you want to be disruptive and a leader, but, most importantly, if you want to excel in your lane, don't try to be something you're not. Fake news does not build a powerful brand; it ruins your brand. Advocate for others by being visible. Invest twenty minutes a day liking, commenting, and engaging on other people's platform feeds. It's the best and most cost-effective way to attract new opportunities and it's called magnetic energy.

Now you may get stuck. I mentored a woman who works in corporate, and she said, "Tory, I'm doing all these posts and I'm trying to build my connections; I'm connecting with others. Why isn't it happening fast enough? Why aren't they coming to me?"

I went on to the activity feed of her LinkedIn, and I said, "It's all about you. There's no advocacy for anyone you're partnering with or creating this amazing magic with for the brands you represent."

And she says, "What do you mean?"

I said, "Rather than posting about yourself, what about posting about your team or coffee dates or the amazing things that the clients you represent are doing? When you switch your thinking, other people will switch their thinking about you and they will see that you are an advocate and want to connect with you because they will see you as a team player who adds value and someone interested in a mutual exchange of energy."

Your positioning, a digital footprint, the way you connect with people, the way you ask for information matter. Whether it's about me, me, me, me, or whether you're like me and it's about a mutual exchange of energy, you want to take people on a personal brand journey with you, because once they're on the journey, they're with you for life. Make sure you understand and appreciate their journey too. For clarity, that's called an energy match!

CHAPTER SIX

Coffee, Not Lunch: The Power of Connection

*"Good people, clear goals, pure intention, and positive
energy are what build forward momentum."*

—Tory Archbold

When I started my first business, the best advice I received was
when I discussed how to connect with others to build reputation,
influence, and advocacy. That advice has served me well. Coffee, not
lunch. Coffee because it is a cost-effective marketing spend, and most
people embrace this morning ritual to kick start their day. Lunch was
deemed expensive because in those days if you asked someone out for
lunch it usually involved an expensive restaurant and an equally expensive
bottle of champagne. My bank balance would agree with this suggestion
despite the fact I was developing and creating my success mindset to

partner with the world's top retail brands, celebrities, and influencers. I knew they wanted that lunch; I had to convince them of the value of a coffee date and at times that was a hard ask as expectations were high in my industry. People wanted to be "seen" and "heard" in the right places.

I developed a strategy as an ongoing weekly ritual to connect with others, anchoring the conversations in a mutual exchange of energy and most importantly in alignment with my values, intent, and purpose. I recognize people are time-poor and you need to give them a reason to want to connect with you and you need to make it simple. I learnt people want to be "seen" and "heard," and if I could develop these wants into a campaign to build a brand and business by tapping into the power of the 2.25 billion cups of coffee consumed in the world every year, I could be onto something. It was an energy mindset.

The strategy was simple. I would connect with three different people per week to build my business and drive conversation, and most importantly, this weekly commitment would be nonnegotiable. I learnt coffee dates are about storytelling and engagement. It's a commitment to lifting other people up, sharing experiences—not just the good stuff, but the challenges as well. I found that people become involved in these conversations and then they become advocates for your business. When you have advocacy in a business, whether in a leadership team or as an entrepreneur, that's where you get growth.

Three coffee dates a week is all it takes to build a powerful global community and this mutual exchange of energy rolls like this:

1. Coffee with someone in my tribe.

2. Coffee with someone I wish to form a partnership with.

3. Coffee with someone completely outside of my comfort zone.

Fast forward twenty years and a commitment to thousands of coffee dates, this cost-effective strategy built my first business and ignited my passion to start Powerful Steps. The only difference with the second business was I had a strong, powerful network of people I had met around the world due to my coffee dating commitment and Nespresso martinis if it was after an after-work "business date."

I learnt the art of a good conversation and leaving a lasting memory from a conversation propelled my business forward. I was not afraid to stay connected, check in to see how they were and send them snippets of information that would be useful to them personally and professionally. I built advocacy while building my own personal brand. Most importantly I believed in what I was creating and that I would naturally attract the right people if my mind, body, and soul aligned with the bigger picture I was manifesting. I never questioned that fact. I also understood my own brand's power and the story that underpinned its success.

Getting Started with Coffee Dates

Be strategic about who you want to connect with by creating a manifestation board of targets. I call this the power of connection and break down my manifestation targets below.

Be sure to get your Coffee Date Lesson video training and step-by-step guide from me in your digital bonuses at selfbeliefisyoursuperpower.com/bonus.

The Three Types of Coffee Dates

Someone in my tribe is someone I am already connected with and want to stay connected to. It is likely someone I have known along the highway of life, worked, or partnered with. I like to keep the connection and memory bank moving. These are people I highly value and invest time in. Should my week allow it I invest in up to three of these "coffee dates" in person or virtually.

Someone I want to partner with—a brand, business, sales, or media pitch. It is a brand or person I feel aligns with where I wish to take my business. I invest time in creating the opportunity for a win-win for both parties because let's face it—we don't have the freedom of time to not get this mutual exchange of energy right. I arrive researched and prepared.

Someone completely outside of my comfort zone. This is where I think *big*. I may be a girl from down under but that is not stopping me from having the power to reach out and connect with others who I feel would empower me to become a better version of the woman I am today. I am not afraid to lean in and ask my community for help in being introduced or endorsed, as I would connect them to the power of my community and connections when they lean in and ask too. Why? Because I trust the connection and they trust me.

Why Should These People Connect?

This involves working on your own personal brand, so you make it easy for the connection to say yes to the time and energy you are asking them to commit—we are looking for an "energy match." This is where the facts of Captain Google come into play. Take a moment to Google your name or business and consider what it says. How is your personal brand represented online? Do you like what you see?

In our programs, I ask others to do this, and these are the crazy results. A woman in leadership with a team of twenty Googled her name and the first thing that came up was she was a drug dealer from Idaho. In fact, she worked for a global pharmaceutical company and was responsible for generating millions of dollars in revenue. A cofounder of a business magazine who interviewed and profiled the world's top CEOs was a bridal expert. A high-profile private banker was a shoe—I asked a simple question—was the shoe flat or high? We had to make light of the situation because a) He was male, and b) If you want to become a power player and build global connections to step into your power and build your business, what Captain Google says about you truly matters as perception is your reality.

It was time for these people to shift the world's perception of them and take control of the narrative. Mahatma Gandhi said it best: "Be the change you wish to see in the world." I remember so clearly an acupuncturist handing me a handwritten note with these words, which I keep in a journal for reference because it's true. We must first recognize who we are and make the changes we wish to share. This means stepping into our power and owning who we are to shine a light for others.

Representing yourself online means you must clearly understand who you are and what you offer. This is the law of attraction and what I like to call "energy on a page." You can shatter the myth that success results from hard work, plans, and ambition if you discover the power of energy fields. When we manage our inner power source with greater awareness, anything is possible, and investing one hour in discovering who we are through the simple act of self-love and discovery can make a difference. Your title or what you do for a living is irrelevant. What is relevant is the power of your story and how you choose to translate that story so that you can step up and add value to others in business and life.

If you're in business the quickest way to build brand SEO, a.k.a. your online digital footprint, so that Capitan Google celebrates you rather than defames you is to start a profile on LinkedIn. It drives SEO and, if I'm honest, 30 percent of my business referrals come from advocacy on this platform. It is a great referral to my website when we share relevant, empowering content. I consistently invest in getting my profile aligned with who I am and what I stand for and I am not afraid to change it as I evolve, learn, and grow. It acts as a business super attractor, and I will share how you can make it yours.

Pick a Venue Everyone Wants to Experience

When you connect for a coffee date, pick a standout venue. You want to invite your connection into a high-vibe environment which means doing your research before you suggest where to meet. No matter where I am in the world, I always ask—where is the best coffee and what's the hottest cafe near the media or corporate hub in the CBD. On business trips to New York and London, I pack Tim Tams (an iconic Australian choc-dipped biscuit, which is hard to come by overseas) and give them to the concierge, which helps get the "real" coffee date insights! That way you are "in the know" even if you feel like you are in a new environment. Remember there is always a solution to a challenge; you just need to reach out and ask.

By asking these simple questions, you are in the driver's seat of where to ask your connection to meet you. My Sydney favorites are Bills in Bondi and Kimpton Margot in the city. My LA, NYC, and London favorite is Soho House and not only do they create the best coffee, but they also deliver the human experience, and I am always "seeing" other people in the same venues, which means I can strike up a conversation and be social, using the time to my advantage. It also helps if your "coffee date" sees people they know too. So, give the venue some thought and start locking in those three coffee dates a week to shift your energy forward and create the space for opportunity and miracles to find their way to you too!

Stay Connected and Follow-Up

Never ghost a connection. If you had the intention to connect, you must have the intention to follow through and thank them for their time and energy. Most importantly if it is a good connection that delivers great energy to your day, propose the next powerful step you can take together. I often call the next day to let them know how much I valued the conversation, or I post something I learnt from them on social media to move the conversation or partnership forward into what I consider to be a power connection worth my time and investment. If you are 50/50 on the coffee date, that's OK too. Be the leader and say thank you anyway. Life is too short, and if you are committed to investing in taking powerful steps forward, you should also be grateful for the opportunity someone gave to create the time in their own busy schedule to meet you and say thanks.

I would also encourage you to take it a step further and if there is any opportunity you feel would be a good fit for that connection, a relevant article to their passion or career—share it with them. Show them you are invested in their journey and your connection. People always appreciate staying connected if you add value to their life. Keep your energy relevant if you are ready to attract and receive new opportunities and *always* stay engaged with them on social media platforms. People will appreciate the time you invest in leaving a comment of gratitude or a thought for them to consider on their post because most people look but don't touch—meaning they scroll and know everything you do but don't get involved—like a fairy tale ghost. I like getting involved and showing authentic care. That's why I follow limited people and constantly unsubscribe to irrelevant content. I don't want "noise" in my feed; I want to engage with the people who matter and align with my values, intent, and purpose. And yes, I trust this prompts you to unfollow and unsubscribe from irrelevant "noise" and unrealistic bikini shots in your feed too.

Say Yes to Lunch

Once you develop a strong network in alignment with your higher self you will notice invitations to lunches and events will start rolling in. From my years at the helm of TORSTAR I understand the true value of what an invitation means and here are the fast facts. People invite you to be part of their event or community because you are of value to them, and they believe you can deliver something special to what they are creating. Every guest we targeted to attend an event for a global brand was invited for a reason—we wanted to build a lasting relationship between the brand and connection to ensure we created an experience they would want to advocate to others without us asking. Why? Because I believe when you fall in love with a brand experience you want to share that experience with others too.

My advice is when you are considered a valuable part of a network and an invitation arrives for you, say yes. Create the space in your diary, make an effort to dress up, show up, and connect with others through sharing the power of who you are and most importantly why you are there to support that business or brand. The universe will start aligning you with the right people at the right time if you take the time to understand and ask for what you truly want. This means feeling valued, seen, and heard within a like-minded community network, the community that advocates for you because they genuinely like who you are and what you stand for. This is called a positive brand advocacy experience and you don't need to allocate marketing dollars toward being a "valued connection." It's a mutual exchange of positive energy that benefits everyone. I also like to say when mentoring my clients for the win—don't be that person who feels they "deserve" to be at an event and bitches about why they missed out. Be grateful to receive an invitation because you earned the right to be included. And always ensure after the event you send a personal note of thanks—events can take months of strategic planning to pull together, with many stakeholders having a say in making it perfect for you. Let them know you value what they have created and what you have experienced.

Once a week during my morning shower ritual, I plan my go-forward coffee dates. One morning I was focused on what podcast hosts I would like to collaborate with and started writing a mental note to myself on who I would like to connect with to make this happen. We had a PR working on this outreach and part of who I wanted to collaborate with was Mark Bouris, host of *Australian Celebrity Apprentice* and a successful Australian businessman who invests his time and energy in sharing business and financial insights to empower others through TV shows, podcasts, and newspaper columns. To put it simply, I loved that he willingly shares his knowledge and is not afraid to call bullshit on the many pitches he is sent and shares his reasons why. He makes you stop and think twice.

My idea for this podcast swap by the PR was rejected by his people—I know how the circle of life works and that didn't surprise me. He probably never saw it. The thing about being a good manifester is you never give up on an idea if you believe it will deliver a positive outcome for others and you understand it will find its way to you when the timing is right—you are open to receiving the miracles of life with open arms. Fast forward a few months and I received a text message from my accountant, asking me to a networking lunch at the last minute. I like and respect her and asked for more details before committing. We are invited as a guest at Mark Bouris's table—he is the guest speaker at a business and wellness lunch.

A few months later he rejected the offer to appear on my podcast yet invited me to be on his. The universe allows both parties to be involved in a mutual exchange of energy. For Mark, I was a perfect match for his audience, yet the timing was not right for him with mine. I was OK with that because when you lead your life with gratitude and understand the power of surrendering to what is meant to be you will understand that what may feel right for one person may not be right for the other. My level of respect for Mark at that moment went up an extra notch for all the right reasons.

CHAPTER SEVEN

The Art
of Delegation

"As humans, we are imperfectly perfect."

—Tory Archbold

I am not a domestic goddess and have a motto in life: "You cannot be good at everything." I'm OK with that. Why sweat the small stuff? Traveling through Singapore airport one year I picked up a book written by Haemin Sunmin called *The Things You Can See Only When You Slow Down*. It's sold over three million copies and has positive affirmations such as, "Don't wait for what you want to happen, act first." Sunmin makes you think about life through a different lens, and he questioned some fast facts about why high schools don't teach us some of life's essential skills like how to cook, go on a date, watch our weight, how to be financially responsible, how to pick ourselves up after a setback, and how to be mindful of our thoughts and emotions. I believe we don't get taught these skills because life is a smorgasbord of discovering who we are, and without the lessons, we would not be who we are today. We need to learn from trying and saying, **"Is this right for me, or do I need help from someone else?"**

I was taught the basics of cooking in high school but likely failed the subject. Cooking wasn't for me. Ask my daughter; embarrassingly, I burnt spaghetti and toast throughout her childhood and still do today—I had to delegate this daily task if we were to nourish our mind, body, and spirit. Growing up, she experienced eating out in different places and, when we got into the rhythm of life, great home delivery or a nanny cooked, which meant more one-on-one time with her, which was highly valued versus slaving in a kitchen trying to get things right. My daughter invested in teaching herself how to cook because I couldn't and, thankfully, I married a man who loves being in the kitchen creating meals too. I would give her an A+ for that and a big hug of gratitude to the universe for him!

It's widely known that people value family, relationships, financial security, and a sense of belonging to a tribe or community. Value is important in life as it informs our thoughts, words, and actions. Our values are important because they help us grow, develop, and create the future we want to experience. Every individual and organization is involved in making hundreds of decisions every day so the question will always come up—what do you value most and what are you prepared to let go of to remain committed to that value? For me, it was simply delegating the role of cook to spend time with my daughter, and now it's time with my husband while he cooks. We enjoy being in each other's company and chatting about what happened during the day with a sneaky kiss here and there.

People always struggle when they launch a brand, business, or campaign and question if what they are creating is good enough. They work through

THE ART OF DELEGATION

a brand identity, which leads to a creative strategy, copywriting process, and launch strategy, bringing all the elements together and then they say, "Argggghhhh, is this OK? Is it good enough? Am I making the right move? Will it attract the right audience? Will I make sales?" So many questions and limited answers because, unless you back yourself and try, you will never know! A fun fact about Powerful Steps? I changed the website four times in our first year of business. Did it affect growth? Absolutely not, because each version I birthed was an elevated version of the business I created and believed in. So, make that move you are thinking about, surrender to the process or experience, and don't be afraid if it doesn't work out because in this digital day and age you can change it in a heartbeat.

As a leader, delegation is important because you can't—and shouldn't—do everything yourself. Delegating empowers a team (or family member), builds trust, and assists with professional development. For leaders, it helps us identify who is best suited to tackle tasks or projects. My affirmation for delegation is, **"Always surround yourself with people who are better than you."** Believe in the possibilities of outsourcing what you can't do, so you can focus on what you can create. Delegation is different for everyone and there is no one-size-fits-all option. Entrepreneur and founder of Virgin Group Richard Branson credits his dyslexia for helping him develop a knack for delegation. He keeps it simple because he needs it simple. With simplicity, it becomes easier to delegate. Founder of Microsoft Bill Gates is one of the richest people on earth and he learnt that successful delegation is about picking the right people, which means hiring people with a slightly different skill set than him. He hires those who take on his suggestions and come back with, *"Wait, have you tried doing it this way?"* to produce an even better product, which is also how he is empowered to position himself as a global thought leader. Warren Buffett's delegation strength is keeping emotions in check by leaving them out of business decisions, believing there's only room for rational thought. Delegation is not "boxed." It is about what works best for you so you feel empowered to step up and shine a light by becoming a better leader voice for change, partner, mother, or wife.

I share a mantra during my programs to get through those self-doubt moments that you can write in lipstick on your bathroom mirror as a daily reminder to shift your energy forward. Simply write, **"I am good enough,"** as when you remember your strengths, forget about comparison, and let go of perfection you will see the world through a different lens. Reading this mantra every morning until you "get it" is a game-changer, and often other family members will see it and start to shift their own mindset and energy too.

Let's tap into an exercise about empowering yourself to "let go" and propel forward in business and life. With the right mindset I find it easier to step up and into my power and know you will too. It's a simple list and, leading by example, I am sharing some of my struggles with solutions.

STRENGTHS	STRUGGLES	SOLUTIONS	ACTIONS
Creating and building powerful brands	Cooking	My husband and daughter love this	Allow them to cook
Seeing the runway of life	Cleaning, washing, ironing	Give this task to someone who loves it or would enjoy adding another client to their list	Outsource weekly
Providing solutions to challenges	"Me time"	Make time to plan my yearly schedule to include commitments to others and myself	Nonnegotiable time booked out in my diary in advance so I can see light at the end of the tunnel when it gets busy
Leading teams for the win	Administration tasks—not great with technology, willing to learn but time-poor	Give more to my team and invest in technology to build automated systems that work for my business	Be clear with my pain points and delegate
Elevating people's consciousness	Saying yes when I have limited time to deliver because I am a people-pleaser	Value my worth, increase my rates, and make myself available to those who appreciate the value I deliver in the timeframe I can commit	Let others know this is who I am and how we can work together one-on-one

When you're overwhelmed, know that your mind can play tricks on you. Don't allow that to happen—it's a nonnegotiable if you want to level up, so always give yourself a silent nudge to switch your thinking and keep taking those powerful steps toward your dream or goal! Remember, you are good enough.

Filling out this simple exercise allows you to lean into your superpowers (of which there are many once you map it all out), allowing you to create space and opportunity to invest in building your powerful brand, business, or leadership skills that others can help you through the art of delegation. Know that there are always ways that you can step into your best self while you learn delegation. These are the four powerful steps you can use as a reminder that it's OK to let go, because if you try to be the master of everything, you will likely fail at the things that you cherish most in life:

1. **Meditate.** Pray or visualize the outcome to activate your infinite potential and manifest your dreams. Utilize the power of the morning shower ritual to start activating what you truly desire today.

2. **Be detached.** Don't let the opinions of others stop you from going after your dreams with all your heart. When people come to dinner at our place and see I can't cook, they are often flabbergasted; some are even rude, while others jump in and help. Do I take on that energy? No. I own that fact and remind them of what I am good at, and (as a side note) we have invited you into our home as we value you; don't judge the way we work as a team.

3. **Start building your future.** Do it alone, do it when you are completely scared, just do what's right for you to fulfill your dreams and ignore the haters.

4. **Focus on yourself.** Compete with yourself and every day become a better version of yourself—take the high road and know that your self-care energy investment will help you fly.

What you cannot delegate is your health or happiness. That is on you to understand that your health is your wealth, and a happy heart is a magnet for miracles. Both mantras fall in my nonnegotiable category and get top priority when I wake up. Our physical capital is our ability to earn a living and make investments. If this was taken away from us, how do we thrive? We can't. Our body is our temple, and my biggest life investment (besides my family) is my health. It's the number one spend in our household as I learnt the hard way when I was recovering from septicaemia after my appendix burst unexpectedly. My greatest struggle was to find a solution and overcome chronic and adrenal fatigue, which drained me for three to four years after an operation to save my life at two o'clock in the morning. I didn't have that get-up-and-go, dynamic ability to be me and it was beyond frustrating as I sought help from many doctors, healers, and friends while getting my head around living differently.

I needed a cure for a disease characterized by profound fatigue and sleep abnormalities made worse by exertion. The fatigue worsened with activity and wasn't cured with rest. This was a lesson from the universe to *stop*. I couldn't even make it past the fifteen-minute mark in a Pilates class before my body caved in. A UK client in Australia requested a meeting and wanted me, not the director I trusted to run my business. I have no idea how I could

SELF-BELIEF IS YOUR SUPERPOWER

drive there and back—it took immense willpower to be "game on." I even had a power nap in the car before I walked into the meeting. The result? A week in bed.

My double life continued as we tried to cover it up as much as possible as my business was at risk if I was not available to lead. I hear stories often about other women fearing judgment if they step away from commitments. When they become sick or face extreme circumstances, they feel they need to keep going because of family and work commitments and are afraid they may lose their job and income—the sad fact is they often do. I feel for them as I know what it means to not know what's on the other side of an illness you are unsure how to fight and who you should turn to for advice without judgment. I know if you keep going, a solution will present itself and you will make life happen how it works for you. For me that meant the basic tasks had to be taken care of. We hired help around the house and I had hair and makeup artists get me ready for client meetings, events, and team milestones, as I wanted to look presentable (at times I felt like a walking corpse). We hired a driver to ensure I got to these commitments and my daughter to school—some days she missed out because I couldn't move, and we cuddled in bed—call me a bad mum but I'm OK with that, as you do what you do to survive.

I learnt how to nourish my body and place it first. I did not have the time to spend another week in bed. How can you lead if you can't move forward? I learnt to say *no* when my body said *no* and here is how I now live free of that disease and in my power.

1. **Sleep allows you to be a great leader.** I am in bed by nine o'clock each night and have a sleep app to track the eight to nine hours I need to rest my mind, body, and spirit. This allows me to retain what I learn, recall information, and stay focused so I am in my power to help others. I also found that sleep allowed me to fight disease and develop immunity and is not to be underestimated.

2. **Stress weakens our immune system.** In recovery mode, I experienced extreme stress through what I was dealing with personally and professionally. That's a fatal mix that not many people can handle. It weakens your immune system and what I discovered is I needed my immune system working for me, not against me, so I started stripping out what I didn't need in my life to create space for what would make me happy and healthy.

3. **Moving your body daily delivers energy to your brain.** I didn't give up on my Pilates class; I went with what my body needed. When it needed rest, I gave it rest. I learnt that small movements become greater movements and improved my ability to do everyday activities so now I can do all the sporting activities I love again.

4. **Fuel your body with goodness.** I started with over thirty vitamins to heal my body twice a day, along with twelve rounds of antibiotics and a threat from the doctor that they would place me back into hospital if I didn't get rid of the stress and negative people that surrounded me. It was broken in every sense. Green juices, broths, and healthy, nourishing food give you fuel. Today I understand what my body is capable of and what it needs. It speaks to me, and I fuel it based on these feelings.

5. **You cannot place a price on preventive care.** Make time for you. Regular check-ups with your doctor—blood, scans, whatever trigger you have in your body is an energy block that needs addressing. Do not ignore it; embrace it, and be part of the solution to living a happy and fulfilled life.

I feel grateful every day that I can be a business coach and mentor to exceptionally talented female entrepreneurs and one of those is Lauren Magers. She's the type of woman who makes things happen and is not afraid to delegate because she is clear on her focus and what she needs to outsource to level up. One day she asked, "What if you could wake up and have the happiest parent and the happiest kids at the same time?" At that moment she decided to create a system that would enable thousands of parents around the world to think and act with love.

Lauren backs herself; she's a risk-taker with a vision and she is not to be underestimated. Broke in her twenties with a bottle of J-Adore perfume she had purchased a few days prior in her handbag, she had no option but to ask for a refund to buy petrol to get her to Las Vegas because her intuition told her something bigger was waiting there for her, and it was. She won the jackpot, met someone who believed in her tenacity and offered her a sales executive position at CBS Outdoor in Los Angeles. Lauren loved to hustle, and most importantly she loved translating the unachievable sales targets they gave her into millions of dollars in revenue—it made her feel validated and good. In record time she became their number one sales executive until one day she decided to open a media agency with her husband Brad, transforming it into a $100-million Fortune 5000 company with a client roster including Gucci, Burberry, Hermes, and Masterclass. There was no doubt she was at the top of her sales game. So why did she walk away? She was thirty-two, had a team of eighty, was burnt out, and had a spiritual calling to heal children and humans to tap into who they truly are. As a mother of four she had experienced blending a family at a young age and then birthing two children and had life experience of the pain points and happy points.

Lauren wanted to shift the parenting paradigm and took some time to understand what that meant within her family dynamics and those of her friends. During this time her calling became crystal clear and that's when our paths crossed as she sent me a DM via Instagram. She had found her life purpose and was ready to birth The Happy Life System, "a blueprint to understand your family's core values and mission by operating as a team so everyone is clear on roles and responsibilities." By taking time out to find her purpose Lauren's family unified and was motivated to contribute and support each other no matter the circumstances. What she created provided the framework to make that happen for herself and others. Now her mission is to create the happiest families on earth, calling this the "Happy Parent + Happy Child Revolution!" And yes, it involves delegation!

When you're in a leadership role, it's important to delegate so you carve back time in your schedule for *you*. Lauren now does this with her family, and I have always liked to do this with my team. Traveling and meeting new people feeds my soul, yet I cannot grow unless I have others supporting my business so it's down to teamwork to truly create the magic, and this is how I do it.

1. **Understand what to delegate.** Not every task can be delegated and to be a great leader you need to be accountable. Writing agency briefs and management of performance reviews need to be *you* as we

are ultimately responsible for the outcome of a project or brief. It comes down to our management style and willingness to be available when others hit roadblocks in the delivery ecosystem.

2. **Play to others' strengths and goals.** We need specific people to deliver specific tasks, as, let's face it, we are human and not built to be perfect.

3. **Provide the right resources.** Make the time to train and give appropriate resources to the person you are delegating to, so they succeed in the task. Before you hire them, ensure they understand your business and what it's like to work with you. It must be an energy match, or the relationship will fail!

4. **Clear communication channels are vital for success.** I use a variety of tech apps such as Acquity and Keap to track project updates and be available for my clients' needs. It streamlines the time I give to each person and allows me to work efficiently and effectively. I don't have voicemail. I found it took up too much of my time to go back and listen to the backlog of messages, so I got rid of it in my thirties. I also make it clear when they work with me that I am not that person who will respond within five seconds of you sending a message. These are the times I check into these apps (Trello, Slack) each day and am available to help you. When you create clear boundaries people either find a solution or value what you have to say more graciously.

5. **Value feedback.** As a leader we can always do and be better. Value others' input into how you lead your team or run your business, as that's

where you gain growth. Give credit and celebrate others' success—life is a two-way street and based on a mutual exchange of energy.

Remember delegating is about creating space for what is important to you. It's about becoming clear on what you value now versus working toward valuing what your future self wants. The best way to understand what you value is to fast forward into the future and visualize what that looks like. During my transformational phase I was lucky to have a mentor in New York who was a shaman and helped me shape what that "future me" looked like. She taught me the power of visualization, a form of imagery and a toolkit that allows us to dream big and beyond the impossible. In moments of trauma it helped reduce stress by propelling me forward to visualize my ideal future. This ritual can also prepare you to respond to a situation before it happens by enabling a positive outcome by conditioning the brain to see, hear, and feel the success or outcome already crystalized in your mind. In my morning shower ritual, I practice visualization for the day, weeks, and months ahead. I save the years ahead for a more focused practice which I call the Dream Delivery Meditation, which I teach others in our community.

To kick-start this process for you, there is a list below of things you may consider valuable or can expand upon to understand the life decisions you will make by creating space for what matters most versus sweating the small stuff and not enjoying the ride of life.

DO YOU VALUE...?	YES	NO
Health		
Family		
Friendships		
Education		
Career		
Volunteering		
Travel		
Life Experiences		
Gratitude		
Spirituality		

I've spoken about my work values (passion, integrity, delivery) attracting miracles and now I will speak about my personal values and how they manifested into creating the family I always wanted.

1. **Health**—Our health is our wealth and without it we cannot show up as our true selves and give to others.

2. **Love**—Unconditional love allows us to be free of judgment and fear.

3. **Family**—Place your arms around the ones you cherish most, and, yes, friends can be family too.

Values are important because they end up intertwined with your own powerful story. They will empower you to understand what you stand for and against. Once you've identified your values, you can then think about how you can showcase those values inside your everyday interaction with others. The sky's the limit when we decide to walk down the highway of life on our own terms, aligned with our value set with the right people by our side.

My advice is to take a quiet moment alone and journal what you truly want. Map it out. Think *big*. Nothing is beyond our reach as we all have the power to create a runway that showcases our purpose and power. If I look back to when I went to Bali and created my first journal in my early twenties, I was fearless about what I believed I could step into and create. Place yourself on top of a mountain, lean in, and feel the freedom of achievement and describe it in words that you can refer to, as this is how you manifest your powerful future. Do not limit your imagination and always remember it takes a series of powerful steps to get to the destination and you cannot do that alone—master the art of delegation. When I look back at that journal I took to Bali, it became reality because it was not about "me"; it was about people, places, and opportunity. It was about a mutual exchange of energy, a powerful tool that I learnt to master.

CHAPTER EIGHT

Delivering Global Impact

*"I love creating and building global brands. Some people
refer to me as a PR powerhouse and super-connector.
I refer to myself as a jack of all trades because I never
want to be boxed—I just want to inspire and empower
others that anything is possible, and I don't believe you
can place a title on that."*

—Tory Archbold

I believe when you love what you do and lead from the heart there are no
barriers to what you can achieve. When I switched career paths in 2019
from agency owner to launching Powerful Steps, I took the key learnings of
that experience to show people the runway of their lives and how to create
and build their own powerful brands. Creating a powerful brand is directly
linked to storytelling—the how, why, and advocacy before it lifts off and
delivers impact. Delivering impact directly results from owning the power

of the brand story—your product, service, or you. Yes, you are considered a brand proposition too!

The power of connection and communication is directly linked to how you represent yourself to tell your story and anchor it to your truth, values, intent, and purpose. The most powerful brands in the world excel because they add this to the mix—they sit back and listen to what people want. They develop into billion-dollar brands because if you can create "listen time" in your daily schedule, you can be agile and create the most exceptional stories on behalf of the brand you represent, delivering an exceptionally good understanding of what the customer wants, needs, and relates to. It's called tapping into the customer's energy, and as every good brand or leader knows, the customer always comes first. They need to believe in the power of that brand and you.

How do you define your own powerful brand story? You make the commitment to invest time in brand you and understand the patterns in your life. I believe there are synchronicities and no coincidences. Allowing yourself to "own" who you are and believe in what you can achieve is a powerful life asset—it's called self-belief and is your ultimate superpower. Remember, building a brand and delivering global impact is about taking ownership of who you are and understanding your audience and their capacity to engage with you.

Every week I invest a day for myself, my brand, and business—it's called a *block out* and nothing will convince me (other than a family commitment or supporting my inner circle of friends) to give up this time. I do this so I am across my business in a way that is truly anchored to my truth, intent, and purpose. It gives valuable, nonnegotiable time to connect with others and play catch-up if it's been a busy week (or month as sometimes we get caught up in the machine of life).

Clients often say they can't commit to setting aside time in their schedule. I always push back because the simple fact is they want to become better leaders, grow their businesses, lead, and disrupt. My question is always how can you do this if you're running in circles without a toilet break in a jam-packed schedule? I get it because that was me once upon a time and, during that stressful period, we had to add to my schedule working out a solution for being constipated because we failed to set aside *block out* time, which was a side effect I don't recommend! Toilet stops cannot be underestimated. Our bodies speak to us, and I should have listened to mine as I was holding excess stress and trauma in my stomach from placing others first, a.k.a. people pleasing, that people often asked if I was having another child! The solution was to delegate what I could and create the space to invest in myself, my brand, and my business, and go to the toilet when I wanted to without someone asking me to place them first. Sound familiar? It's a known fact that men and women multi-task while on the toilet, answering work emails and reading social media feeds to stay informed and have "me time." Make time outside of the toilet to do this, as you will gain so much joy when you align your life without feeling the need to "jam" it all in!

You may be questioning how I can block out this time and still earn an income and this is my advice: *power up*. Know your value to others and most importantly value yourself. Nothing is stopping you from raising your fees or hourly rate. My beautiful client Julie learnt this through an unexpected experience. She was diagnosed with stage III melanoma and needed to create space for treatment and recovery. We had been working together on her brand for a year and I knew she could ask for more, so I gave her a gentle nudge. Raise your fees; those who value you and what you deliver will not question it—they want to work with you because you deliver impact and that's an asset you can tap into. She did and they never questioned the rise. In addition, she created the space for her treatment without the stress of wondering where the business would go while she prioritized her health.

Here is an exercise you can do to create and understand the power of who you are, what your superpower is, how to value it so you can use those powers to propel you forward. You can use this five-point story to create something that captivates your audience or customer. New connections will not remember everything you say; however, they will remember the power of your story, which becomes your gift to the world as you understand the power of storytelling to lead others to deliver global impact.

I recommend you follow these five points below, create a Google doc, and then set aside a few hours to deep dive into your own life story—don't be afraid to be honest with yourself, as that will be your first powerful step in this process. Remember this story is about you, told in your words, explaining and breaking down your life and business experiences. It has lifelong value as it is used as an asset to attract what you deserve into your life as you build out your own powerful brand or business. I use mine daily to tap into the power of my life lessons in TV interviews, podcast chats, and keynote speaking opportunities. I leverage it to shine a light for others to become intent-based leaders not afraid to speak their truth to showcase how challenges will always translate into opportunities.

I recommend creating these five sections in your Google doc for the story of your life:

1. What was it like growing up?

2. Who did you want to be when you left school?

3. What are your career highlights?

4. What was your game-changing moment, a.k.a. your live-or-die moment from the universe, that triggered a change in how you lived your life?

5. Where are you today?

What Impact Can You Deliver?

Now remember, this is your life story, and I don't know anybody whose life story is worth a sentence for each question! Deep dive, let it all out as you will find patterns in each part of your story that you have either broken or need to break free from. Celebrate your success and remind yourself of the challenges you have survived; these are all life lessons that make up the unique power of you.

Here's an example of how the story of my life and this Google doc process unfolded for me that might trigger something in you. When I look back at the power of my five-point story and the twenty years that I spent at the helm of TORSTAR and the brands we attracted, it became clear that it was a stepping stone for Powerful Steps because it set me up for success. I could see in Stage IV of my story (a.k.a. my live-or-die moment) I started to shift my energy toward focusing on what truly mattered, what I was willing to give others and removed the takers. I created *boundaries* and gently shut doors on people not in alignment with what I valued, which created space for others who fit in perfectly. It elevated my energy levels, and I radiated, which meant I attracted better "energy matches" into my life. I found myself in that live-or-die moment, that halfway mark of my life story. I believed in myself, backed myself, and now know and embrace the possibilities that come from viewing challenges as possibilities.

My friend and entrepreneur Jose Bryce Smith also believed in creating a global business through the power of her personal story. She created Original Mineral because she saw a gap in the market for ammonia-free hair color. The brand was born from a hair salon she started with her then-partner, where she served as a receptionist while she dreamed big. On my podcast she spoke about being a receptionist as "the hardest job that I've ever done in my life," yet it created her business idea as she created a solution out of a challenge. The fumes of hair color in hair salons twenty-two years ago were fierce as they could burn your eyes and harm people who had scalp sensitivities; many hairdressers had eczema. She thought there must be a better way for people to look and feel good, so she set about creating possibilities by developing and testing products.

Through her story, there are clear game-changing moments where you can see how she embraced her situation to propel herself forward with passion and pure hustle to translate her dream to build a world-class brand into reality. Her ideas started coming to life in the salon she managed downstairs, while she lived upstairs with her then-partner. To put her situation into perspective, they had no kitchen or bathroom, just a toilet. They would shower daily at the pub down the road and lived like that for two years, never telling anyone choosing to fuel their passion with determination and sheer hard work until they could afford to move out. After many false starts, a marriage, two children, and a divorce, she cracked the formula and it did amazingly well. To get to this point she had to continuously back her dreams through the power of self-belief and at times to survive re-mortgaged her house. "I had put everything into it. I was even selling my clothes online for extra money. I needed to get a big order from a US distributor for the business to survive and he had had my last product, which hadn't worked that well. He was sceptical about reordering because he'd been through a lot with the one that had had a lot of problems. He basically ignored me for about three months. I went through Facebook, Instagram, phone calls through his EA and he ignored me solidly. In the end he messaged me, and he said, 'Are you not going to give up?' "

Jose owned it and said, "I know that you had some problems, but I'm telling you this is a world-class product."

And he said, "OK, I'm going on holiday to Bali; you have to come and meet me there and you need to bring the product."

Jose had been told many times, "We love your product but who owns the company?" She found being a woman created barriers to growing her business. This time she switched her thinking and called a male friend and said, "Would you come with me on this trip and say that you're on the board of Original Mineral and look after finance?"

He said, "I don't even know anything about your business."

She said, "That's OK." And he came and did that for her, helped her save her business as the distributor purchased a million dollars of product up front and signed a contract for four million. "That was a moment for me where I just absolutely had to hustle because my house, everything I had was on the line and I just couldn't give up—that was probably my biggest breakthrough moment." Jose 100 percent backed herself by providing a solution and asking for help to break through the barrier to her success. Original Mineral is now stocked in fifteen countries around the world and boasts year-on-year growth of around 30 percent.

In business I deal with a lot of people who suffer from imposter syndrome. It's a feeling that you don't deserve your job despite all your accomplishments, and you hold back from taking risks for fear of failure. It can affect anyone, regardless of job or social status, but high-achieving individuals often experience it, and women in leadership roles experience it most. I am always blown away hearing the stories from women in our programs who don't feel they are good enough or are worthy of that promotion or pay rise when they create their five-point story. I always say, never devalue how far you have come and what you have achieved. What is the worst thing that can happen? They say no? What is the best thing that can happen? They say yes!

Let's take Sally, for example. She is the CEO of a brand generating millions of dollars in revenue, and it was clear when she developed her five-point story her retail career was determined when she was twelve—after a long and frustrating shopping expedition with her mother. Exhausted and empty-handed, she decided she would make a difference—and she did. I found the power of her career story extraordinary—the challenges versus the opportunities. There was one constant—she was not afraid to step up and make things happen. When she told me she was at a crossroads in her life and didn't feel valued, I advised her there were two ways she could look at it: start again or show others your value. Become visible and get people who have had positive experiences with you to advocate for you, and most importantly create boundaries that work for you. Sally went from employee to business owner within a few weeks, negotiating a hefty pay rise and equity in the business she led. Her story's power showed she delivered value, and they were willing to acknowledge it.

You can also deliver impact through the simplicity of how you sign off an email showcasing the power of your story and what you stand for. No doubt you have received a lot of emails throughout your life. Ask yourself the question. What was the most powerful one? For me it was from supermodel and spiritual seeker Rachel Hunter as when it landed in my inbox, she simply chose three emotive words: love, truth, and grace. On an episode of the *Powerful Stories* podcast I asked her why.

> Love obviously has this fierceness within it because love is strong. It is so strong. It's this magnetic field that we have, and this is what we want in our life. Just be in your truth and that is not someone else's perception of truth. It's your truth, right? So, then we go to grace and be able to listen and to be in a state where you

are receptive, and you have the ability to be gracious and in gratitude. There's a softness. So those are really where those three words came from. Because you can't sign off on a shitty email when you're signing off on Love, Truth, and Grace.

When I switched from "TORSTAR Best regards, Tory" mode into "Powerful Steps Much love, Tory" mode, people questioned why I would sign off an email like that to men *and* women. My answer was why not? That's how I feel; I am connecting with them at that moment and I don't want it to be formal. I want them to understand this is me, raw and real. The truth is I wanted to surround myself with people with happy hearts and to have a happy heart you must first understand the power of self-love to create and deliver an impact that holds value for others. Self-love can be a tough topic to approach. It is when you replace criticism and comparison with acceptance and appreciation. It's valuing your opinion and not sacrificing your well-being to please others (a.k.a. the toilet stops). You can find self-love by owning the power of your story, the good, the bad and the ugly—own it all because it is your legacy. Once you accept who you are it will set you free and the miracles of life will start to appear. You will appreciate the simpler things because you know and appreciate the true, soulful version of yourself and are not afraid to remove yourself from situations and life patterns that no longer serve you. That is why my emails always end with a blessing of love to those I connect with, as I want them to lean into my energy fields and propel forward in business and life, knowing they are loved.

When investing in self-love and self-care, signposts will start finding you as they have for many others. After a long hiatus of investing in health retreats and the incredible mentors and experiences that come with them, I was able to return to the magic of Kamalaya in Koh Samui after lockdown. Despite my jet lag, I attended an early morning yoga and stretch class. I am not that stretchy or agile; however, I decided that to get my body moving, I would need to give it a good dose of self-love and care. The miracle appeared in the form of appreciation for what I had gifted my body and the message delivered was a caterpillar making its way gently across my yoga mat. In its metamorphosis, the caterpillar becomes an exquisite, winged creature in the form of a butterfly and is a metaphor for transformation and hope, affirming the number one reason why I came to Kamalaya—to write this book as a symbol of rebirth and resurrection so that others can unleash their self-belief and make it their superpower. To me that's an example of global impact, striving to make the world a better place by healing others' minds to understand if they believe in what they want, they can shift the energy forward to make their wildest dreams possible.

How Do You Share the Power of Your Story to Attract Success?

You anchor everything you communicate to your truth and energy fields. Do not be afraid of judgment; sink into the moment and just go for it, like the CEO of a Southeast Asian luxury brand portfolio. It was during the global pandemic he discovered he had cancer and on LinkedIn had taken his shirt off, which—let's face it—no one ever does, let alone a CEO because it is considered taboo when you are a corporate leader. He took his shirt off to showcase the cancer scars all over his stomach from the surgery to save his life. I was blown away by his authenticity and rawness because when I had dealt with this man, he was very business-like in terms of getting things done in a polished manner. When we worked together, he was a powerhouse in a suit, and I was the powerhouse's publicist delivering the message to launch the global brands in his portfolio. Seeing him in that vulnerable situation and showing that vulnerability to the world encouraged me to check in all the time. I wanted to learn more and no doubt others did too.

By sharing the power of his personal journey and how he invested in his success mindset, his style of leadership became clear. He had taken people on his journey through a global business tool, LinkedIn, just like you would a product or brand—only this was his own personal brand. When the time came for him to launch another "actual" big brand in Southeast Asia, he came back on LinkedIn in a suit and said, "Thanks to my team. My support group did it." And I thought, *Wow, this is just for me.* This is a standout because you're being vulnerable, authentic, and you've taken people not only on your personal journey but as a leader you lead. In business you have a team that has your back. You've now over-delivered on the business outcome that everyone wants to be involved in. It was brilliant storytelling by a CEO who showed true vulnerability and authenticity in a time of turbulence for himself and the world.

How Can You Deliver Impact?

I will answer this question on what does not deliver impact. I recently engaged an agency and was assigned a leader to manage our account. By week five of a twelve-week project working with her she had not picked up the phone to engage with our business, learn more about us as a brand, or build a relationship and did not return any calls, only making herself available in the weekly WIPS. The girl who reported to her was the opposite. While less experienced, she was passionate and willing to learn. She called, texted, and was engaged in our business. You could see her daily views on our social media channel, which was why she could deliver impact and hit her targets while her leader failed on what were considered higher yield targets and became defensive when questioned how she represented our brand. I concluded this was not how I wanted my business or brand represented and pulled the pin on the project. The agency then decided it was not how they expected leaders to lead; she was asked to leave, and they pulled the pin on her too. What happened to the less experienced yet passionate leader? She was headhunted by a larger business where she believed her passion would be recognized and decided to move too.

To be a great leader you need to lead by example. People only follow, and your business will only gain momentum if you are invested in the everyday experience. You do not have the choice to "step in or step out" when you are in a team or business that relies on the power of human connection. It's all in and game on, or choose another career.

Why place yourself in a box when you can make someone smile somewhere in the world because you have stepped into your power and are not afraid to deliver impact? Think about the caterpillar and its point of evolution—of course, it wants to transform into a magical butterfly. A butterfly has wings and can fly, which brings more opportunity and joy to its life journey. It doesn't want to gently plod along the highway of life, avoiding people who may squash the life out of it (by accident or on purpose). The mindset of the caterpillar is if it can conquer the obstacles and challenges, it knows its life path is to create and deliver a bigger offering and it will. The caterpillar will 100 percent step into its birthright and destiny.

The point of evolution is to think and dream *big*—nothing is impossible with the right mindset and an investment in daily rituals like the morning shower ritual, journaling, meditation, walks in nature, or an inspirational podcast or book that allows you to gain a different life perspective. When you learn to surrender to receive and forgive to trust, the signs of life will find you and you will claim that dream sooner than you thought possible.

Follow the signs to find the possibilities of the impact you can deliver by creating the time to slow down and looking for the evolution meant for you. Many years ago, on a trip to Japan with my daughter Bella, we arrived in Kyoto. I hadn't had the time to research where we were going and trusted my assistant and travel agent to book an "incredible experience" for us. On reflection, if I were standing in Kyoto today, I would have made the time to understand it is home to numerous Buddhist temples, Shinto shrines, palaces, and gardens, some of which are listed collectively by UNESCO as World Heritage Sites.

During this time, I lived a fast-paced, jam-packed life and being digitally connected to my business was essential (or so I thought). I was responsible for creating and launching powerful brands around the world and let's face it—the career I had chased in the media didn't stop for anyone. I had trained myself to be available twenty-four seven—the one who would provide the answers and, if people asked me to jump to make their campaign happen, I jumped as high as I could to make that a reality. To place this into perspective, in my early years of TORSTAR I used to set an alarm clock for three o'clock in the morning to wake up to walk down the street to buy the newspapers on a Sunday morning so that when my clients woke up in various parts of the world, I could inform them what had been written about their brand and CEO. I was dedicated to the business of pleasing people.

Kyoto is a magical part of the world and unknown to me; we were about to step into that magic and become present in life as we were placed where we needed to be. You could feel the slow pace and simplicity when you walked the streets. Most of the places we ate at did not take credit cards, only cash, and it felt like we were in a time warp.

Clearly the universe wanted me to *stop*, slow down, and follow the signs. I had to listen to my inner voice to seek the answers because the hotel we were booked at gave us two options—go on a boat up the river to check in or take a two-person car up a road that fit two people if you walked it. We chose the boat and I was so frustrated because it was *so slow*, and my daughter said there was no internet. We were heading to the Hoshinoya hotel in Arashiyama along the Oi River, which gradually narrows until Kyoto's city landscape is displaced by a world of seasonal, incredibly rich colors in the form of its landscape—the boat trip took fifteen minutes and it felt like a lifetime. I was frustrated, agitated, and disconnected. Slowing down was a lesson I needed to learn.

At the hotel we kept seeing the number 111 everywhere, which I now know is **a sign of enlightenment**. It also represents self-love, abundance, and good luck. We walked to our room, overlooking the Oi River with two single mattresses placed on the floor to sleep, no TV, no internet, and what we considered at the time as essentials for a hotel experience. I would say the universe hit us with a privilege versus entitlement moment as it was time to relearn what life was truly about when you slowed down on expectations versus reality as we had the sound of the river flowing, birds tweeting, and our own company to fill our days and nights with no distractions. The meals and how food was consumed was simple. Tea was a ritual to be enjoyed. The experience transformed our thinking, and we embraced the beauty of what was in front of us—nature and our family unit.

Talk about evolution. We had no choice but to embrace nature and the gift it was to deliver. We leaned into the power of conversation, walked and talked our way through the Bamboo Forest, and learnt to enjoy the fifteen-minute boat rides in and out of town or walking the winding road to and from our home for the week. On these walks together I started to hear the secret whispers of life and that 111 kept appearing made me inquisitive to learn more about why this number was in front of me. It became clear; a transformation was coming, and we were placed in this magical part of the world to step away from life as we knew it to understand there was more to life if we simplified the way we lived. This experience did not change me overnight, but it got me thinking and opened a new energetic gateway of "being present" while being a single mum and heading up an agency delivering global impact. I learnt the art of balance through the power of nature and slowing myself down to receive and believe in the wonders of the universe. I also was not afraid to delegate more or hire more people so I could give more time to myself and the journey I was embarking on. The gift of this experience was personal evolution so that I could evolve. I was given the space to think and create, understand how I could share the gifts I was given to the world, and now understand the power of nature as one of the greatest known healers that will always guide us to the next transformational phase in our lives.

Powerful Stories with Impact

Sometimes transformations come in unexpected ways, and you cannot prepare for them. I came across a post on LinkedIn from Christine Vance, a talent and people leader in Dallas, and the power of her story moved a needle for many people around the world as it went viral.

She wrote:

> This week marked six months since I lost my husband and father to our four young children due to complications of COVID, including the misdiagnosis of Multiple Myeloma. I had seven days with Andre prior to him being placed on life support. After fighting for ten days, the Heavens welcomed him with open arms.
>
> Throughout this journey, I have been reminded firsthand of the importance to focus time on family, health, and passion. Over the past two years HR professionals have worked tirelessly to ensure our people are safe and cared for. What many of us did not do was follow our own advice. Remember, take moments for your own well-being, and make memories with loved ones.
>
> I am at peace with my situation and look forward to my next opportunity in our new future.

It was an incredibly powerful narrative, as in her thirties she became a widow and primary caregiver of their four children. I checked our common connections and noticed she had worked at Neiman Marcus. Years prior, I had the privilege of working alongside creative innovator Ken Downing and the communications team to launch the brand in Australia and it was one of those partnerships I truly cherished. I reached out to her, introduced myself, and asked if she would like to share the power of her story on my podcast. We met for the first time on her birthday and the podcast interview was a gift to herself and the children.

When we spoke, the power of her story had over 80,000 likes and reached over three million views within forty-eight hours. Through this devastating experience she learnt to be vulnerable and transparent, yet "did not let myself, a lot of times, just be in my feelings." She was focused on being positive after the post went live and tried not to see underlying stress from the trauma she had been through. Christine realized the point of her post was that in the working world people have stress and that this life challenge placed her at a crossroads. By viewing the crossroads as a transformation, it empowered her to pivot and see "what do I need to do to make a less stressful environment overall for my health, for my children, and for the world, to be the best person at work in whatever I do next." Part of her legacy will be this post, as it was a pivotal moment shared with the world and it left an impact. Never be afraid to share the power of what you are going through, as someone somewhere may need to hear your story to see their challenge as a possibility too.

By becoming present and following the signs of life you can follow this mantra, which I simply love: "Don't think local; think global." You are likely thinking, how can I deliver global impact? The answer is simple. By showing up and being present on social media you are already a "global citizen" because anyone anywhere in the world can find and connect with you. By understanding the power of your five-point story there will be a common thread that you can share on these platforms on what has driven your success and how that unique gift has underpinned how you lead and connect with others in times of success and survival. Through your very own story you will see your personal brand runway through life experiences—use these to deliver impact on social media platforms, speaking engagements, team leadership meetings, or within your own business model. This is how you will understand the value and unique gift given to you at birth to shine a light for another. Christine learned this lesson too and became an inspiration to others through her heartbreaking experience.

In the programs I host, this is the biggest breakthrough women have—discovering they are worthy of receiving global abundance. In the words of a senior corporate leader who positioned the outcome perfectly, "Having the courage to own my story and be OK with it showed me I can own my power." Coming from a remote or different part of the world, they think small, as if they are only relevant to their local community, *but* the truth is they have signed up to learn and discover more. I always say to them, "You signed up for something bigger than you know. Let's unleash it." They walk away knowing they can have a global mindset because they learn from their story that they have personal power and can use this power positively to enhance lives in business and life, no matter where they are based.

I had a powerful podcast chat with David Meltzer, a legendary sports executive, entrepreneur, investor, and speaker who has partnered with millionaires, billionaires, and impactful leaders. He found his purpose simply because his wife called time-out when he was running the most notable sports agency in the world, which gave him access to things that even billionaires couldn't do or afford. David had been lying to himself, surrounding himself with the wrong people and ideas. In his words, "All of a sudden, my wife, as I came home at five thirty in the morning after lying to her [and] partying, told me she wasn't happy, told me she was leaving me, told me to take stock in who I was and most importantly, what I wanted to become. That moment changed my life because I had no idea. Because nobody was telling me no. I always say, be careful of all the people that say yes to you and surround yourself by the people that give you the radical humility to know that you don't know what you don't know." So "although I was upset with my wife when she told me at first that she was leaving by the next day, I realized she was right. And I realized that I don't hate her or my dad, my mom, my friends in the world of blame, shame, and justification. More importantly, I hated myself."

David made a pledge after that moment with his wife to help over a billion people become happy. Now you can't make a pledge like that until you become happy. His wife called him out and he had to admit, you know what? I don't like myself. How can I find that inner happiness? How can I find the true essence of David and rise to make that pledge?

As he explained, "It was not easy. It took sixteen years to live up to that pledge. I don't believe in limiting myself. I started with my values and my values started with gratitude. And so, when I realized that gratitude would give me perspective, it had given me perspective and it would be to find the light, the love, and the lessons in everything that I did. I started with simply saying thank you before I went to bed and focusing in on all the things, I was thankful for and thank you when I woke up. And that changed my whole life. Then I moved on to, to forgiveness, which gratitude gave me perspective, but forgiveness gave me peace. See, that's where that paradigm shift came in, that I was at ease. Finding the light and the love allowed me to be more inflow, more at ease, allowing me to believe there's something bigger than me, an omni mission, all-powerful knowing source. The third value was accountability. Now that's evolved over the last sixteen years. It started with what did I do to attract this to myself and what am I supposed to learn from it? But there was a punishment element involved as I look through certain traumatic situations in my life that I, when I was nine years old, was abused. So, I as a nine-year-old did something to attract that to myself. So, it's evolved to something more powerful. It says, what did I do to participate in this perception of others or me?"

David then looked at his life story and asked, "What am I supposed to learn from it? When we take accountability, we now have control by surrendering. I have perspective, peace, and control, which led me to the final value of effectively communicating. And it's not just effectively communicating with others to empower them to be happy. But effectively communicating with source. How am I utilizing fear to either get me up, get me started, get me back started? Or how am I using fear to get outta my own way? And that effective communication, that ease then created these values that led me to accelerating the trajectory of what I think I want. Now all I had to do was evolve daily practices to execute on those." And that's how David found his purpose and life gift, which not only lifts him, but most importantly others around the world.

You might be questioning *What is my life gift? I am struggling to see what I can offer.* We all have an "offer" that can be viewed and an "offering," and when you take the time to dive deep into the power of your five-point story to focus on self-love and self-care, the patterns you see within that Google doc will jump out at you in bright shiny lights. Your ultimate superpower will emerge and become crystal clear. Most importantly, you will understand the deep meaning of who and why you are here. The answer for me is always this—my life gift is to deliver impact to the best of my ability with love in my heart. I like to bless each experience and connection and most importantly bless the future me, the one constantly learning and evolving because I understand the true power of a happy heart being the magnet for miracles. Without my happy heart, all I attracted was trauma—it was clear in my story. That was the pattern that needed to be broken and it never got repeated because I chose happiness over fear and judgment.

Think about it like this: reading the words on this page are already shifting your energy and mindset forward. You chose to make the investment in purchasing the power of these words because you are looking for change, a better way to step up and into your power. Right now you should thank yourself for making that power move and most importantly thank your future self for the powerful steps you know you will take to move forward, as somewhere in this book there will be a trigger point, an aha moment, when you say, "I can and will do this," as you know deep in your heart you are ready to spread your wings and become the butterfly. Most importantly, be willing to find and understand your unique gift and global footprint by committing to the inner work of your personal and professional story.

We can deliver global impact in many ways and often it takes a game-changing moment to recognize we have the power to make it happen on a larger and grander scale. I interviewed entrepreneur Camilla Franks—the Australian Kaftan and resort wear designer who took her brand global with authentic endorsements from Beyonce, Paris Hilton, and Jennifer Lopez. During the global pandemic she stepped into her power and believed, "It's those big moments that make us shift into Wonder Woman gear for survival. That's when we grow to our potential."

For Camilla, lockdown was a game-changer. She built a global business she refers to as her "brand baby," then COVID hit and the domino effect of what that meant for her business was huge. Who would laze around the house in a fabulous silk kaftan as she wisely stated? Well, some of us would do that, but for most of her customers buying a kaftan in extreme times didn't make sense. She stocked in fifty-five countries and had over two hundred stockists all around the world who suddenly cancelled orders, sending millions and millions of units of stock back. She found the experience overwhelming, as she was also responsible for over two hundred tribe members (who she calls her angels) who were ultimately her work family.

In our podcast interview she explained that it was one of those "Oh God" moments. "How am I going to fix this? My CEO and I, and my head of finance, are amazing. I wouldn't have survived if I didn't have the exact team that I do because I'm not great at the finance or legal stuff. Operation's not my forte. I made a promise to myself, a contract to myself. I didn't want to make one redundancy through COVID. I didn't want to lose one of my angels to this, and I wanted to keep my stores. I lost Bondi. She was collateral damage. But we worked tirelessly to keep the band together. But for me, that was terrifying, the thought of all those years, that blood, sweat, tears, day, night heartache."

She recalled there was one beautiful moment where they pulled a lever and said, "We've got to try and save people's future. I've got a lot of single moms in there—these jobs matter. So, we did this online warehouse sale. But because of town hall, we couldn't have a real one. We had to do an online one. So, we all came together, barcoded, scanned, price coded over eight thousand units. We put them on this online sale, and we had a big monitor at the office, and we could see 50,000, 100,000, all this money. And we knew every 100,000 was saving another job, saving another job, saving another job. We were all holding each other's hands crying and screaming, popping champagne, knowing that we saved ourselves for another three months or six months. We ended up getting to the end of the sale and we ended up doubling the profits that we would have in any normal sale. So that was a big aha moment. We talk about duality in life. Like there's crappy moments in all that stuff. But there's also the beautiful stuff. We never would have done that. We've got to recalibrate. No one wants to wear silk with crystals in lockdown."

I am sharing the power of other people's stories because you have your own powerful story. You need to own it and share it to deliver the impact. Someone somewhere in the world might be waiting for their own sign, their calling, and you are 100 percent responsible for granting that gift and that is how miracles appear—by others shifting their energy and momentum forward by staying true to who they are and what they value. If you're feeling vulnerable about sharing that story, reframe your thinking. I don't often talk about the hard times I faced on socials because I am focused on the future, not the past. Hard times happen, and they happen to everyone, which is why at some point in your life when the timing feels right, it is important to share them. If I am honest, I always feel vulnerable sharing the tough times in my life (yes, even in this book!) and when a podcast interview I did with *Those Two Girls* shared their thoughts on my most vulnerable moments on socials, my heart skipped a beat with the headlines:

- **The Grim Reality of Her Glamorous Life**

- **Why Keeping Her Family's "Dirty Little Secret" Nearly Killed Her**

- **What Was Really Going on Behind Closed Doors and The Steps She Took to Transform Post-Trauma**

Then I saw the first comment from a mother and businesswoman in Queensland, and she wrote, "Just finished listening, I loved it. It must be one of my favorites, left me feeling happy," and I knew I did the right thing because when we own our story, we own our power, and that means we can empower one another.

CHAPTER NINE

Be True to *You*

"You are only in your power if you know who you are
and are happy with who you face in the mirror."

—Tory Archbold

You're not rich until you have something that money can't buy—for me
that is happiness. It can take years to find that elusive trigger point
before you find it. Trust me, I know. Life didn't fall into synchronicity until I
entered my forties. I took a long hard look at who I was and what I wanted
from life to make tough decisions to get that breakthrough and find a sense
of well-being, joy, and contentment. Statistically people feel happy when
they are successful, safe, or lucky—for a long time I did not feel safe and
was operating in fight-or-flight mode, so it eluded me, and I had to own that.

When fifty years old, Jennifer Lopez expressed learning, "The journey of
becoming whole on my own" was her most valuable life lesson that made
her discover her own true happiness. "I always thought I was going to find
happiness and love and that another person was going to give that to me,

and then I realized that's not how it is at all. You get to be happy all by yourself. If you can appreciate yourself and know your worth and value, you can be a happy person." I get it—we need to stand in our power and own who we are. Why waste hours worrying about other people's opinions or waiting for someone to validate us when we can focus on producing our positive self-worth and fulfillment?

I relate to J. Lo because, when my manifestation came through and I won full custody of my daughter, it was a breakthrough moment that I thought would make me happy. Instead, I cried for hours—a release of twelve years of trauma and the keys to freedom to live life on my terms. My friends kept saying, "Tory, now you can finally date, live your life, and have some fun," but I knew myself better. I needed time to heal my mind, body, and spirit. I needed to get to know the new me and what she wanted from life, and it took six months to find her. That made me whole; it made me happy. This was when the magic of life fast-tracked, and miracles started appearing at every turn because I chose to live life on my terms and never questioned the belief that I would find happiness and it would find me.

Let's put into perspective the journey to happiness. Yes, it can be awkward. I placed myself in some uncomfortable situations, like the time I went to a "Happy Meditation" one night in Thailand hosted by Sujay Seshadri. I liked the sound of being happy, but didn't know how to be happy and this meditation sounded like a good start. After the group settled, he asked us to do our best belly laugh, the type when you have deep gratitude for yourself and everything that you choose to surround yourself with. He showed us his, and here is where the self-judgment, self-worth, and every other feeling along the lines of "who is watching me" came into play. I found it hard until he said, "Many people have come before you and found this hard. I have

BE TRUE TO YOU

watched them become awkward and look around the room to understand if this is how others are feeling too." He said the trick is to own your belly laugh, let go of judgment, and enjoy the freedom your body truly wants by allowing it to give this miracle of happiness to you. Well, the room gave it everything, and I have never laughed so hard in my entire life. It created this ground swell of, *Who gives a fuck about what I look and sound like? I am doing this. I am owning this, and I am becoming this.* At that moment, a major energy shift propelled me forward.

Let's talk about entitlement versus privilege because it goes to the core of what makes us happy. Privilege is the ability to access certain things others cannot. Entitlement is the misconceived belief that you should be able to access those things regardless of your circumstances. Nine out of ten times, the way people go about getting what they feel entitled to is wrong. This is such a valuable lesson for us to learn. What is it that we are entitled to versus what is a gift or a privilege? I believe when you feel entitled to what others have you will never find inner happiness, and instead you lean into your weakness, which means you will never unleash your true power and potential because you lack self-belief as the creator and director of your life journey.

Self-belief is our ability to complete tasks and achieve goals. Having self-belief (like my daughter Bella showcased when she pursued her music dreams) means you understand you are capable of success, which activates your chance of heart-led success. Those who feel entitled to success are led by ego and reduce their chance of success simply because they believe they are entitled to have what others have without putting in the hard work. These people lack self-confidence and usually have low self-esteem yet want to prove they are the "king or queen" amongst their peers. To become the king or queen of life, the one thing that we can turn to is choice, which means we can fix our attitude into a win-win mindset with the confidence to believe that we are enough and one small powerful step forward can lead to change. If we are willing to grow, adapt, understand our strengths and weaknesses, we will step into and own our power.

"Be true to you, even if it means riding solo for a while. The right people and opportunities will find you eventually. Show up for yourself as that is all that matters."

—Tory Archbold

To own your truth, you need to know exactly who you are, understand your worth, what you stand for, and most importantly how you value and know yourself. The first step to knowing yourself is to truly love yourself. Oprah says it best, "You feel real joy in direct proportion to how connected you are to live in your truth." This means embracing all your strengths and weaknesses, not being afraid to take ownership of who you are. The hardest part of anchoring ourselves to our truth is disconnecting from what we were taught in our family system while growing up. For many of us this means do not question the status quo, live in denial of what you truly feel and put on a happy face to the outside world even if you are broken inside. To break away from patterns that do not serve your higher purpose is the hardest thing you will ever do, but when you understand the power of trusting and believing in the miracles that come your way because you choose to be anchored to the truth of your values, intent, and purpose you will understand the power of who you truly are. This will become your greatest life asset.

An example of entitlement is a man who feels he is free to take from others simply because he lacks the self-belief to make the funds to be the hero and live the life that he feels he's entitled to live. He wants to be the king but does not believe he has to work hard or hit rock bottom to understand the life lessons to create his kingdom, so he chooses to take from others to build a false kingdom.

Entitlement Versus Privilege

In the United States, Bernard Madoff, creator of a sixty-five-billion-dollar Ponzi scheme, takes the title of being the largest investor fraud ever attributed to a single individual. He was once the toast of New York society and often described by the media as hardworking and the busiest man on Wall Street due to his role as chairman of the NASDAQ Stock Exchange. He was "busy" because he had too much to cover up and was living a lie, believing he was entitled to it all.

How can you step into your power if you believe you're entitled to what others have created? This is where karma comes into play, because when you don't have a value set nor understand your life purpose, you operate in a low vibrational world where the choices you try to hide eventually catch up with you. That was where Bernard's story ended— with a 150-year jail sentence.

I will give you an example of how this has happened to me and how I learnt to forgive the situation by understanding that forgiveness is the key to a happy heart. Most importantly, I understand that this happened because the person lacked the self-belief to create their own kingdom.

A few years ago, a friend whom I cherished greatly turned a blind eye as her husband reached out to me to invest in his business. I was a single mum and when he reached out my cash flow was tight. I had downsized my business to focus on resolving a family law court matter and every dollar mattered because my priority was to put food on the table and pay for my daughter's school fees, as the private school system gave her the structure she needed to thrive in a tough situation. I gave him funds to invest and had to continuously chase him for the paperwork and updates on where the money had gone. After a few weeks of no paperwork, I asked him to return the money as realized investing in his "fund" was a bad move and he was not to be trusted if he could not honor the investment with the paperwork required, given it was an ASX-listed company.

Instead of returning my investment, he took his targeting and sense of entitlement to the next level. He became desperate and asked if he could have access to my superannuation (retirement) fund, plus assets and liabilities to invest in an even bigger fund he was creating. Among his varied requests was if I could bring my passport as proof of identity and meet him at one of Australia's most reputable investment companies with a relative, a high-profile banker who worked there, to "endorse" the transfer of my funds. I was interested to see where this deceit landed so I went along with it as his wife had told me he was having great success with this "business."

He became nervous. He knew what he was doing was wrong yet couldn't help himself because he felt entitled to the gains he would obtain if his plan worked out. Ultimately his goal was to become the king and build a kingdom without doing the work. He couldn't have planned his aura of success and deceit in a more perfect setting—the two of us standing, overlooking Sydney Harbour in a prestigious and reputable banking office where high-performance directors are known to deliver extraordinary results. This man, my friend's husband, asked me to invest my hard-earned retirement fund into this bank with his relative as a conduit, under the disguise it was for his business portfolio. This was without accounting for where the funds I had already invested had been spent.

I believe a miracle entered my life that day. The relative never showed up and my friend's husband looked like a fool trying to track him down on his mobile in the bank's reception, leaving frantic messages and no doubt texts asking where he was because without him there was no deal. In his eyes, the money he felt entitled to take for his "kingdom." While waiting in this plush reception area, he kept trying to pitch me other ways to invest in his company, making it clear that I was not to discuss this with his wife. How uncomfortable for both of us and how dare he place me in that position because he knew what he was doing was wrong.

Had I not trusted my gut instinct, believed in the magic of miracles, and followed the signs to see what would unfold, I would've lost close to a million dollars that day to a man who felt entitled to what I had worked hard to earn. Fast forward to 2022, and we woke up to an Apple news alert that he had been charged with four counts of fraud and dishonesty in Perth's Magistrates Court, resulting in himself or others gaining an advantage to the value of $636,000.

His sense of entitlement was his undoing, but the life lesson is there is no fast way to make money. The foundation that you build in life based around your values, intent, and purpose is what energetically attracts abundance. Losing $20,000 to fund his "lifestyle" is a small price to pay for the gift that they gave me. The power of self-belief ensured I never questioned where do I find the funds to pay the school fees because I knew that gap in my bank account could be translated into millions of dollars if I kept my head, heart, and mind focused on the end game which was to strip out energy vampires like that from my life and only surround myself with people who believe in a mutual exchange of energy.

That valuable life lesson taught me that if you want to attract abundance in life, be true to you.

Attracting Abundance Without Entitlement or Privilege

Here are six powerful ways you can shift your energy and mindset to attract what you deserve without entitlement or privilege.

1. **Begin and end your day with gratitude.** What are you thankful for? I like to do this in my morning and evening shower ritual.

2. **Dream *big*.** Anchor your dream with your truth.

3. **Alter your mindset.** Understand there is no shortcut to getting what you want.

4. **Construct an empowering reality.** Manifestation boards are a great way of creating a series of powerful steps that lead to the ultimate life experiences.

5. **Appreciate the reality of your situation.** Become aware of what you do have versus what you don't have.

6. **Commit to change.** Remember, a small step is always a powerful step; don't be afraid to take one.

If you choose to implement these powerful steps, you will start to live by a beautiful inner knowing, trusting your gut instinct and the spirit that comes through you by loving yourself first and your life will flow. You'll view challenges as possibilities because you are anchored to the truth of who you are. Those that stand up and switch on their A-game will use that philosophy and thrive—they believe they can, and they do. They also understand the power of what it means to "be true to you."

CHAPTER TEN

Nothing Is Perfect: Success vs. Survival

"A crisis is necessary to challenge us and force us forward to accomplish what we are meant to step into— the better side of us."

—Tory Archbold

I n the past, I've been besties with overwhelm. You probably have too. Reaching to check emails the minute your eyes open, madly trying to get everything done at work before it's school pick-up, worrying about cleaning the house and filling the fridge and booking a wax, and—oh yes—trying to find ten minutes to return a friend's call. Once I was so overwhelmed running a business, being a single mum, and dealing with nonstop harassment from an ex-partner, I had a panic attack on a plane. Before take-off, sitting on a jam-packed flight, I asked them to return me to the terminal pronto. The answer from the pilot was a firm **no** and I had to learn how to manage my overwhelm on a twelve-hour flight. The advice the airline hostess gave me is the advice I am giving in this book—journal your feelings, write a letter to your future self or the ones you cherish and love most, and you will feel a sense of immediate calm and clarity. On that flight I wrote a letter to my daughter, telling her how much I loved her and all the things I cherished about our relationship. It helped calm me along with the kind hostess who kept checking on me, saying, "You've got this."

Typically, we feel overwhelmed due to an accident, a natural disaster, or witnessing a crime. Other common reasons for feeling overwhelmed are life changes that take time to process, such as going away to school, breakups, divorce, a new and challenging position at work, and bereavement. This book is about being brutally honest with yourself about what you have experienced so you can conquer the fears surrounding that pain, release them, and set yourself free from what holds you back. The good news is we are all blessed with an internal superpower to heal ourselves as trauma is stored within our organs, tissues, skin, muscles, and endocrine glands. These parts have peptide receptors that let them access and retain emotional information. This means your memories are stored in your body and brain, meaning you can reframe them when the timing feels right for you. Just remember, your emotions are the vehicle the body relies on to find balance after a trauma—with the right mindset, a big dose of self-belief and a community who supports you anything is possible.

Let's deep dive here as I want you to be brutally honest with yourself because in this book, I am with you. That's the way a mutual exchange of energy works and that's how you can own your story to own your power. I experienced trauma as a teen growing up in a family of conditional love with parents who hated each other. The sad fact is they still hate each other, and it had a knock-on effect for each of my siblings. Trauma then found me in my thirties when I was threatened with serious physical harm by my ex-partner, who not only threatened to kill me, but he also used our daughter as the weapon of communication on how he would do this, which led us to be out of the range of what is considered a normal life experience. This led to feelings of hurt, terror, fright, panic, and edginess for me and my child during a fundamental stage of her life when all she wanted was two parents to parent her.

During the worst times in my thirties, I hid behind a closed door and less than five close friends knew parts of what was going on. I was terrified if I spoke about the true scope people would not want to be my friend or it would end up as gossip at dinner parties—the judgment factor was at full throttle and it took a lot of courage to wind it back and not give a crap about what others thought of me during this time. I have no doubt I was the topic of many lively gossip-filled conversations as I withdrew from being social, focusing 110 percent on providing a stable environment for my daughter, giving her the support she needed to navigate the challenges, and building a business that would provide for us. In my thirties, I lived "out of body" and never felt fully present in any situation, as I was always looking over my shoulder to ensure we were safe and my daughter was OK.

The good news is that part of our life is over because we can rewire our brain—at a point in time the universe will say *enough!* Do you want to live in trauma for the rest of your life, or do you want to live? Do you want to see the miracles that surround you and follow the signs for freedom in your heart to ultimately attract the internal abundance you deserve? That feeling that your heart is so full of love for yourself and others that trauma becomes a distant memory because you have learnt the art of forgiveness for your situation.

Think for a moment about your game-changing life moment, marinate in the experience for a few moments and feel all the feels. It will help you see the light while you read on. For me that moment was when I caught septicaemia and learnt to live again on my own terms, surrounded by the right tribe to rise like a phoenix from the ashes and step into the next part of my journey. It's not to say I won't have any more learnings or challenges, because I know I will—they will keep coming for me as they will come for you. My mindset simply shifted, which means I embrace the challenge because I know I am going to lean in and learn from it. I choose to feel every pain and own it. With a simple reframe you will find your solution. Lean into the challenge and say this affirmation: "I am doing this, I am owning this" every day when you wake up and experience it in every part of your body and then release it at night before you go to sleep. Forgive it and move on.

People who have experienced deep trauma and have chosen to move forward are often the ones who learn the art of surrender and forgiveness, finding it easier to protect their energy from those who do not deserve their time. They often go on to share the power of that experience on the world stage through TEDx talks, writing books, giving keynotes, and mentoring others, because they know if they shine a light to focus on what they went through, it will touch the heart of another and make a true difference in someone else's pain. To place this into perspective, from the moment we're born, we cry simply because we are birthing a new moment in time. Birth can be a painful, transformational process, but know this—stress and pain are necessary for us to grow and develop. Crisis is necessary to challenge and force us to move forward in a more positive, high vibrational way to accomplish what we are meant to step into—the better side of us.

Success and Survival Stories

American entrepreneur Stephenie Rodriguez was pigeonholed as an archetypal Sydney socialite when she moved down under. The *Sydney Morning Herald* said she was a "work hard, play hard woman with a shoe collection to match." On September 29, 2019, her life radically came to a grinding halt on a work trip to Africa. She contracted cerebral malaria—a rare, fatal form of malaria with a 2 percent survival rate—that nobody thought she would survive. On top of that diagnosis, she contracted septicaemia. You could half that 2 percent survival rate and call time on her life. But Stephenie had a positive mindset and during a *Powerful Stories* podcast chat, she shared why this mindset transported her out of her deathbed and back into the world as an in-demand augmented public speaker.

How did she do it? By cultivating her mindset. From "waking up as patient XYZ on my bracelet, unable to take myself to the toilet, unable to move, having no sense of agility and dignity. I was nobody's mother. I was nobody's partner. I was nobody's friend. I was nobody's leader. I was just patient with XYZ on my wristband." She always wanted to see and do things quickly yet through this experience she learnt the value of setting micro milestones, otherwise known as baby steps, with the bionic legs she was given to save her life.

She calls herself "augmented" as "I don't like the label disabled because of the 'dis' part, because that would imply that I am less of a person because of a change in equipment. Someone can get a pacemaker and we don't call them disabled. They have a new part. They're augmented. They're different from their original equipment. When somebody gets a hip replacement, we don't call them disabled. They got new equipment. I have new equipment, I am augmented."

Entrepreneurs will always have success and survival. If you've backed yourself to step out of a corporate role, it means you lose a guaranteed income. Fiona Jefferies started an all-women agency that has created over a thousand sales office designs for blue-chip property clients, including Stockland and Lendlease. She started her business at her dining room table with five thousand dollars as she wanted to find her own path. What her clients didn't know was that while she was building her business, she had a shadow point where she thought of ending her life. She lived in ways that were unsustainable, had trauma growing up, and lost her partner at the age of thirty to suicide.

On my podcast, she talked about this time in her life, how she didn't deal with the trauma as she was focused on building a new business. She kept going and thought, "Yep, I'll get to that one day." Well, trauma can only be kicked down the road for so far and then you've got to deal with it. "I'd been living my life so focused on work, not sharing what I was going through with friends and family that could offer support. Turning up to therapy, just box ticking, rather than doing the internal work" landed her in a position where she found herself attending a Property Congress event and walking through the park on the way back from a gym session, thinking, "Yeah, when I get back, I reckon this is it and the end." She wanted to end her life because she had not faced her greatest inner fears.

Thankfully her therapist had put a suicide prevention hotline number into her phone, as she was concerned she wasn't OK and there would come a point that she would need help. Fiona dialed that number, and they gave her life-changing advice. "You need to think about the next hour. That's all you need to do. You just need to get through the next hour. What are you going to do?" Luckily, she had a friend living near the property event who ran a couple of bars. She rang her and said, "Can I come around?" Fiona believed in the process for the first time and went to see her and cried for what seemed like hours. Her friend sat with her, and it was "the greatest gift that she could give me because it was just a presence. She knew enough that I was in a lot of pain and a lot of anguish, and she was just present with me. She wasn't trying to fix things. I think from that point that just got me to the next hour, and then the next hour and to where I am today." Fiona has successfully run her business for over two decades and recently found her soulmate. She is firmly in our community and someone I cherish as a friend because she owned the power of her story and anchored it to her truth to find her purpose and survive a tough time.

When you find your power, you will no longer be overwhelmed. Each experience that finds you will deliver a gift, which is understanding another layer of yourself like Stephenie and Fiona. By following the signs, miracles always appear; you need to join the dots on the sequence forming for you (not to you) to learn another lesson or uncover another pain point in your body that needs to be released to level up to your next life phase.

Let's revisit the caterpillar story. A day later, I saw butterflies and I knew a transformation was coming but I didn't know it would be an unexpected experience that led me to a place of great gratitude and appreciation for others. I was focused on writing this book, and my mind was ticking and coming to life with the possibilities that the stories shared would create an opportunity for someone to know it is OK to step out of their situation and feel empowered to take powerful steps forward to find happiness and freedom in their heart.

In my own thoughts I tripped on a rock and stubbed my toe. I didn't lose balance or focus; it was a jolt from the universe saying *stop* because when I looked down at my big toe it was bleeding so brightly and with such flow I had to consider, do I sort this out myself or do I ask for help? I walked down the rest of the stairs, blood freely flowing out of my body, leaving a little trail behind, and I said to myself, I need help. So, I asked for help and was taken to hospital to have a tetanus shot and clean the deep wound. Being in a foreign country and knowing I had a book deadline to meet, you would think I would panic because I couldn't walk and had to rely on others to assist with basic tasks. Instead, I felt immense gratitude for the kindness of others and my situation because I knew deep down the universe was giving me the signal to stop attending all the activities that were on offer, focus on myself and the birthing of this book, and most importantly, address some trauma I had been holding inside, because my success and survival story is never over. There will always be new twists and turns in our lives each day. It's how we choose to look at challenges and release the pain or trauma we may be holding onto that sets us apart from others. Our willingness to do the inner work is what makes us whole. To not address what is holding you back only sets you back.

I believe in asking for help when you hit a roadblock in life. It wasn't always the way I lived life, but it is now. I ask because I know someone somewhere can help demystify the energy block we are facing and show us the runway possibilities we can move forward on. Lucky for me, I had a life coach session booked to release an energy block holding me back. My parents divorced over thirty years ago and the way they speak about themselves and the children they birthed is toxic. Toxic in a sense that no matter the situation they will always say something nasty and insincere about one another in the presence of others. If you ever watched *The War of the Roses* with Michael Douglas and Kathleen Turner in the famous scene at the bottom of the staircase when they destroyed the room and each other with such venom, you will understand what I am saying. It's not nice. I chose to break a family pattern by creating boundaries where I was prepared to share my energy and it was not in those types of situations. Lately I was struggling with the fact they are both getting old and felt a familiar guilt, a.k.a. people-pleasing trait, creeping in. Am I OK with that? The answer was yes, I am OK with my decision, but I needed permission to own that, validation I was on the right path, which is why it's always a powerful life tool to lean into the wisdom of others and ask for help.

Through a powerful visualization journey, I realized I cannot fix another person's journey if they are not willing to fix it themselves. In life we have a choice: do we want to be with toxic people and fulfill societal expectations just because they are our family, or do we choose to live with freedom in our hearts because we know there is a better way forward?

Here are five powerful steps to consider that will allow you to create the space to understand who you truly are and what you want from life.

1. **If you're feeling stuck, create a positive mantra to counter the painful thoughts.** The more you rinse and repeat the power of where you want to go, your energy will shift away from your negative situation.

2. **Invest in doing your "own work."** This means understanding what patterns you need to break to get to the next level in life. You will find when you invest in working on you and understand your trigger points you will feel a sense of freedom to walk away from what no longer serves you by creating space for new and exciting opportunities to find you.

3. **Be gentle with yourself.** Don't expect an overnight miracle to happen because it won't find you until you're ready.

4. **If you're in a situation that is causing you pain, accept that the other person may not apologize.** That's OK. Remember that's their story, not yours. You cannot "fix" someone, but you can fix yourself. Forgive the experience and walk away to embrace other opportunities. You don't need to sizzle in a shit pit for one more moment of life.

5. **Engage in self-care.** A happy heart is a magnet for miracles. If you want to attract miracles make the time to receive them. Take time out in nature, go for a run, book a massage, and switch your phone off. The secret whispers of life will find you and you will be grateful you took the time to stop and listen to thrive.

Overcoming Trauma
with Movement

Sujay Krishna, a meditation and life enhancement mentor I value greatly, suggests we start recognizing we have a rational mind and an emotional mind. When somebody goes through anything that triggers great fear or trauma, our emotional mind overpowers our rational mind, and we feel overwhelmed and helpless. Brain scans of people in these states show an overactive amygdala and more activity in the brain's right hemisphere. To process any experience, we need the help of both hemispheres. Talking about it is one way and reexperiencing the situation is another. To support deeper processing, it is important to train our brains to relax. We can relax the emotional brain and activate both hemispheres of the brain in one practice. Sujay recommends alternate nostril breathing in pranayama to be highly effective in bringing balance to your life and processing trauma.

You can also try taking up a sport that empowers you throughout your transformation like Jo Gaines, corporate leader, tech innovator, single mum of two who is a powerhouse when it comes to corporate life. Jo has always been passionate about seeing others succeed against the odds simply because she has lived through a traumatic experience and embraced the bright light at the end of that tunnel. Her corporate life came crashing down when her partner left her while she was pregnant with their second child. She found herself three months pregnant and facing parenthood alone, working full-time with a three-year-old, and in the process of facing her reality, lost her power. After her second daughter was born her partner decided he wanted to come back to the family. During that time and through many more years of being constantly insulted and mistreated, she had lost herself, but she had not lost hope. She finally left the relationship with minimal personal items. She felt stripped bare, yet she understood the power of small steps becoming powerful steps and chose to reclaim her identity and self-worth by learning how to cage fight, which was 100 percent outside of her comfort zone. Leaning into this new skill set helped her stop making excuses for being herself and gave her the confidence to back herself. She says, "It gave me strength in body, mind, and spirit. I realized that mental strength was important and what I needed. I've always been strong in body but lacked self-belief, confidence, and openness. The power of believing that I could take a punch, even step into it, was transformational."

Through the power of stepping into the unknown, Jo figured out how she wanted to be seen and known. What is my personal brand? Who am I? She discovered that what mattered was helping others who are at risk, marginalized, or lacking confidence or self-belief. Our paths crossed at a workshop I hosted where she was encouraged to step into the power of her own story and not be afraid of the narrative. She discovered "my story is powerful," and through the tool kit we share in this book Jo could express it. As Jo sums up beautifully, "The world needs more vulnerable, compassionate servant leaders who recognize the value of their impact and purpose." The next leadership chapter for Jo is about how she can spread this further, bringing the next generation of leaders up with her. What an inspiring way to own your story and power and share it with others.

CHAPTER ELEVEN

Culling Your Tribe

"Stay close to people who want more for you.
Not more from you."

—Tory Archbold

Have you ever noticed when people walk into a room and instantly light it up with positive energy, others naturally gravitate toward them? People gravitate because they want to lean into the positive energy that radiates wherever they go and they want that for themselves too! People radiate when they understand who they are and their life purpose. They are not afraid to look in the mirror and take ownership of who they are by facing and conquering their internal energy blocks, so they can step into their power by serving in leadership roles or building powerful businesses that support others.

Place your hands in the air now if you want to be that person. Feel the freedom that simple movement gave you by placing down this book for a moment and saying yes to new beginnings by shifting your energy forward and upward. That means you are a committed by the simplicity of your action to shift your destiny in a new and exciting direction. With simple movements and mantras, you are clearing old energy and signalling to the universe you are ready to embrace change. To move powerfully forward and deliver global impact, you must consistently clear and be aware of your energy so that it's free of anything that may have attached itself during previous life exchanges. Clear energy is something I cherish, protect, and value and it starts with who you choose to surround yourself with.

Success comes from being brave enough to maximize our potential by creating space to streamline parts of our lives to overcome negative influences, including those we hang out and invest time with. The hard work and acknowledgment of that ambition starts as you read the power of these words which are setting up your intention. Time is a precious, highly valued resource, determining our present and future selves. If you want to achieve goals and live out your dreams, time management and being aware of who you share your energy with is critical, as, once it's gone, it cannot be brought back. How and with whom you spend time needs consideration. Maybe it's time to understand who your true "real life" tribe and cheer squad is so that you only surround yourself with positive energy. A happy heart can find you in record time when your vibrational energy is at an all-time high, which means you will be lighting up every door you walk through!

Choosing your tribe wisely means understanding that friendship, family, and professional relationships are built on a mutual exchange of energy. Life is not a one-way street, yet we sometimes find ourselves in relationships that operate like that. It's important we take the time to appreciate the relationships we have and the relationships we must step away from. At times we may feel that we need to give to receive yet that is not how the law of attraction works. When we give to the wrong people, we become the ultimate people-pleasers and they become the entitled friend, family member, or professional that we have allowed to take from us until someone blows up out of anger or resentment. Anger because they want more from us, resentment because they give nothing in return. I have propped up various people throughout this lifetime and I take responsibility for my part. I wanted to help them, but I enabled bad behavior. One of the most powerful tools in my kit of life was to understand the power of exchanging energy with the right people who value you for you. I will be sharing this tool kit to attract your ultimate tribe during this chapter, and you will notice an immediate shift in the type of people you attract by following these powerful proven steps.

We want to attract the best possible energy in this lifetime, which means we need to do the work on ourselves to become that energy we wish to attract. If you look at a life example in which you attracted "bad energy" or "unjust circumstances," how were you feeling? Depleted, rejected, excluded, ignored, unwanted, taken advantage of? When you met someone incredible, how were you feeling? Happy, excited, adventurous, in love with you first and foremost, right? We must understand the power of what it feels like to love ourselves to love another. The power of attracting "soul" matches also means not being afraid to say "no" to what no longer serves your higher purpose. If you're always traveling up a one-way street, you will never receive the gift of internal happiness. A gift we can all participate in is to create happiness and mutual exchanges of energy wherever we go to collectively raise the vibration of the world we choose to live in.

When I spoke with Marianne Williamson, one of the greatest spiritual leaders of our time and a woman who is not afraid to own her own power, about how to create happiness she described it like this: "We're on this earth to love one another, but that's not what the thinking of the world puts out there. We are assaulted constantly twenty-four hours a day by a stimulus of ultimate meaninglessness. It's almost for the sake of a consumer society. We are taught continually to value things that are ultimately valueless, and we make false gods of things that are in fact not what will bring ultimate happiness. This takes a toll on our soul and we have a very difficult time feeling deeply comfortable in a world that tells us that the unimportant is important and that the important is less important. As we begin to realize that the purpose of every day is not to go after it the way the world teaches us, but rather to show up as best we can as good people, loving people, asking what's ethical, asking, what's good asking what will help serve the world at this time? That's the only place where ultimate happiness will come from."

I'm excited to share this powerful tool kit with you to dig deep, so be brutally honest with yourself to seek answers. This means taking ownership of true thoughts, not the thoughts you feel you should have.

How big is your tribe? My core tribe is less than ten people and I call on them for support, advice, and direction. I have known them for many years, and we have each other's backs. In many ways my friends have become family. We have made the time to understand and know each other, most importantly we support each other when times are tough. We don't judge or walk away and choose to confront challenges together to make things work. Have you ever heard the mantra, "Your vibe attracts your tribe"? Whoever created it was in their power as your tribe is important; it directly reflects your values, intent, and purpose for life. When you're out of alignment with that, you end up facing unexpected challenges, and when you are in alignment, your life skyrockets to the next level. My tribe is a major part of my success, and as you read on, you will come to appreciate that your tribe has contributed to your success too.

One of the easiest ways to determine your tribe is to understand whether you are vibrating at a "high frequency" or a "low frequency." Pay attention to how you physically feel when you wake up or walk into a room with others who are expecting to share your energy. First impressions count in the law of attraction, so if you feel light, energized, clear, and healthy, chances are you have a high vibration and are in alignment with your life purpose, attracting others who also feel this way. If you feel sluggish, experience a mental fog, or are choosing to invest your energy in problems rather than solutions, chances are you have a low vibration. To vibrate at a high level to attract miracles in life means alignment with the right tribe and for this you may need a life hack! A life hack empowers you to recognize and remove toxic energy before it comes into your orbit, dragging down your frequency levels by creating powerful boundaries that protect and preserve energy.

Three Powerful Steps to Protect Your Energy

1. **Own your power and don't give others permission to steal your joy.** When we host programs with high vibrational women, I

make the time to ensure that everyone is there for the same reason, and we have no "victim" mentality in the group. One person can bring down the success of others who are there to rise under your leadership, so don't be afraid to say no to the "victim." A great leader recognizes the right mix of people to deliver impact and the ones they need to leave out of that "mix." Do not take on that victim mentality energy—if you do it will zap you and you will not be able to deliver to the best of your ability. The same applies in a corporation when you're hiring an employee. Energy matters—research what makes them tick and happy so you can tap into the power of that energy to grow your business and allow them to be recognized for their contributions.

2. **Don't give air to what winds you up.** We all have a trigger point, and some people are that "trigger." In psychology a "trigger" is a stimulus that causes a painful memory to resurface and can be a sensory reminder of a traumatic event, including sound, sight, smell, a physical sensation, or a certain time of day or season. I like to conserve energy and avoid exhaustion by simply not being available for people and experiences that do not contribute to my happiness and have become more fearless with my approach over the years due to circumstances. Harsh but true. I value who I am and what I give to others; I no longer have time for the takers.

3. **Stay positive by always finding the upside in every situation.** If someone is not taking responsibility for their own life, don't make it your issue. I like to remind myself, "Their life. Their story. Their opportunity to shape the outcome." As an empath, I have strong insight into what others need, and it can be tough to walk away when others are struggling. It is our role to help where we can but there will

come a point where you need to use the power of walking away to empower them to step up and find a solution. Remember, we are not their solution; they are. You cannot do the hard yards for others, but you can shine a light and show how you got to your "happy place" so they can see the possibilities that lie ahead.

When you wake up to this non-negotiable daily mantra, "A happy heart is a magnet for miracles," you will find that you begin to understand the power of loving yourself first. It can be a tough mantra to live by, especially if you are a people-pleaser. After twelve rounds of antibiotics and no clear way forward to beat septicaemia, that was the best advice my surgeon ever gave me. Medicine was created to cure disease, but the facts also point to happiness being a cure. A strong heart is a happy heart. A happy heart will vibrate at a high frequency, attracting other happy hearts and better opportunities. Your happy heart can work to your advantage and will gently remove negative people from your life, meaning everything you touch, feel, and see becomes possible. Be fearlessly willing to step into your power and put yourself first to capture the heart meant for you. That's how I met my husband—it was an energy match of two happy hearts coming together because our frequencies aligned. Sounds simple; however, sometimes it's not. You need to work on yourself as a priority and address the hard stuff you may have buried deep inside and may not have acknowledged. Unless you understand and address what is holding you back you will not be clear on need versus want. A need is something necessary to live and function. A want is something that can improve your quality of life.

Mantras to Attract High Vibrational People

Breaking down needs versus wants in a relationship we choose to surround ourselves with is simple. Here is a mantra to attract high vibrational people into your life that match the beat of your happy heart.

I want to surround myself with...

◊ **People who accept me for who I am**

◊ **People who are there for me during the good and bad times**

◊ **People who celebrate life with me**

◊ **People who encourage me to chase my dreams**

◊ **People who value and make the time to see me**

◊ **People who will tell me the truth even if I don't like it**

◊ **People who love me unconditionally**

Mantras to Remove Low Vibrational People

And a mantra you can use to remove low vibrational people from your life:

I choose to remove myself from....

- ◊ **People who are controlling**
- ◊ **People who are competitive**
- ◊ **People who are draining**

- ◊ **People who are a bad influence**
- ◊ **People who are two-faced**
- ◊ **People who don't understand a mutual energy exchange**

Assessing Your Tribe

Do you have the right tribe by your side?

My secret life sauce is aligning with who I choose to surround myself with. It's about living in my truth in alignment with my values, understanding my intent, and living purposely. You too can live like this and attract what you deserve, because it's based on a non-negotiable mutual energy exchange. To be clear, that means gently removing the "takers" from your everyday life and creating space for the right people to naturally come into your life orbit. It also means surrendering and trusting the process, which people find hard to do. My advice? Stand in your power, stay true to what you believe in, and trust Divine timing, as you will be grateful you didn't try to "fit a brief" just to "fit in." Trying to "fit in" only zaps your energy and it never truly "feels right."

Let's start with a pen and paper. Get out a journal and break down the important people in your life into three categories—friendship, family, and professional. Limit each category to five people only—people who are your ride and die and are there for the high and low moments in your life. They don't judge; they accept and are willing to pick you up on a deserted highway because you called them for help or to brainstorm a solution. Be brutally honest with this list and remember just because you were born into a family doesn't mean they are the right family for you.

These definitions may help work out who is on your list.

◊ **Friendship** is the bond between two or more people who want to engage with one another. It involves having mutual interest in each other's thoughts, feelings, and experiences. Friendships work on reciprocity of trust, respect, emotional support, and admiration.

◊ **Family** is one of the most loosely defined terms in the English language; it means something different to everyone. While one person may define family as the relatives who share their home, another may consider family to include extended relatives residing near and far. Families are vastly different, but they all function under one premise: shared love, trust, and commitment.

◊ **Professional** are social groups linked by a leader, shared purpose, goal, or common culture. It can also include a business coach or mentor you may lean on for support. These people are important for your professional growth and want to see you thrive and prosper.

I always ask everyone to stop at five people for each of these categories because if we are truthful with ourselves—out of that possible fifteen—it's usually about eight or nine that we can rely on, and these are the people we want to invest our time and energy into. I call them the "lifers" and are the ones we hold close to our hearts. When you are doing this exercise and writing down your names for each category, trust your gut instinct, listen from within your soul, and follow the signs of what that mutual exchange of energy has delivered for you both. Is it a one-way or two-way street? If one-way, they don't deserve to be on that list! Think about it like this— there's nothing wrong with taking a break from people. It's like fasting; you're taking a break to find peace and purpose. If you fill your plate up with shit, you're not going to want to eat it, and neither is the person next to you, so choose wisely as these people will affect your frequency and ability to translate dreams into reality.

Remember—love is not all that you need. To function in a relationship you also need respect, time, reassurance, happiness, and a best friend. You never want to be held back from waking up with a happy heart out of obligation and resentment so be clear on your tribe by being brutally honest about who is in it so you can gently shut the door on an experience, relationship, business, or professional decision that no longer works for you and always say goodbye with grace and gratitude. Remember, you're creating space for new and exciting beginnings. Why hold space for something that is not serving you or is not a mutual exchange of energy? Get that pen out and sharpen your list so only the best of the best is who you invest your go-forward time and energy in. Now, imagine what you can create together to make a difference in this world with no negative people holding you back.

I also do this simple check-in with my husband at the start of every year, and it's based on what we value most as a family unit. We work through who we have truly enjoyed spending time with (who is aligned with us and on a similar path) and want to spend more time with as we highly value those relationships. We then have clear boundaries around what we want to do with our time and energy as our family always comes first. This means the time we invest in friendship and professional relationships is extremely valuable and, at times limited, while our children are in their final stages of school life where they need our support the most. What matters to us at this moment is that they create wings to fly in life, which means our time is invested in empowering them to experience life and all the lessons that come with it. We want to be there when they fall because we know with the right tool kit, they can pick themselves up and fly to the next stage of their life. Outlining what we want helps all our relationships flourish as when we speak our truth, build each other up, and as we connect more deeply, we create powerful partnerships that last a lifetime.

When you understand the power of the people you surround yourself with, the systems you put in place to protect your energy, you empower yourself to view that challenge as a possibility, propelling you forward in business and life. Become protective of what matters to you. Human connection, feeling valued, and partnership bring people together.

FRIENDS	FAMILY	PROFESSIONAL

Move your energy forward by becoming clear and focused on who you want in your tribe. Create space to see those you value and commit by giving your time—on a coffee date, at a dinner party, morning walk around the park, or simply being at someone's side as they battle a challenging health or personal issue.

The Power of Stepping into Someone Else's Shoes

What kills a soul? Exhaustion, secret keeping, and image management. What brings it alive? Honesty, connection, and grace, which is why the power of the "right" connections makes the world go around in life and business. Strong, healthy relationships are key to our emotional, mental, and physical well-being.

SELF-BELIEF IS YOUR SUPERPOWER

You now have the right tribe aligned with your future self. These connections you have outlined, value, and will nurture will equip you with strategic support to find fulfillment. Without the power of "our people," we cannot reach our greatest potential.

Like you, I am who I am because of "the people" I choose to share my energy with, and in business you are only as good as the people you lead or work alongside. The good news is we have a choice on who we wish to share our energy with when we give ourselves permission to release what does not light us up to create space for what does. This can often be a tough process as we gently release relationships that no longer work for us, as sometimes it can be a struggle to communicate the *why* in person without making the situation a greater toxic mess. A positive and powerful way to release these karmic bonds is by being grateful for the opportunity to spend time together, the memories created, and the lessons learnt. You can choose to do this in person or energetically—the choice is yours. You can choose to feel empowered by your decision to move forward and surrender to the process, trusting that if they are meant to find you again in this lifetime, they will, and it will be completely fine. We aim to wake up each day with a happy heart, and you're now on track to attract those miracles as you should be aware of what lights you up and brings you down.

In business you may be faced with a "difficult" person in a "toxic" situation— or so someone says when handing a project over for you to manage. They made that judgment, and you have a choice on how to deal with it. A long time ago I was working with a high-profile celebrity and was told she had one hour to attend a brand launch—and to be wary, she is difficult to deal with so don't speak to her in the elevator as she is just there to "do her job." I found this approach and pre-judgment nerve-wracking. It lacked soul and felt like a monetary exchange, which would translate into low vibrational media coverage, so I decided to research her "day in the life." She was over-committed and had a lot going on in her personal life, which they failed to acknowledge in the brief. I ignored the advice and placed myself in her shoes by meditating on what this would feel like and simply asked, "Are you OK?"

She replied, "No."

So I said, "Let's make this hour work for you, not against you, and give me a nod when it's time to move your energy on. Even if we only make it to the forty-five-minute mark, we will do our best." I was the first one she thanked on a press tour in a long time. My approach was simple—you never know what's going on unless you make the time to learn. When you learn the insight, you can help, and people appreciate that fact.

Power Up with the Right Connections

I mentor others in corporate leadership roles around the world who lead teams of over twenty, and they struggle to keep connected while meeting the demands of their business and home life. Email and Zoom have become a curse, as they lead a life behind the scenes instead of front and center, where human connection delivers more possibilities and opportunity for growth. One of the first questions I ask in a leadership mentoring session is, "How well do you know your team?" And the answer is always top line; they can never deep dive into what makes each person tick, which is why I recommend they start connecting with others through the power of three coffee dates a week for thirty minutes each. The shift in their thought process is immediate as after a few weeks they become alive in their answers when I ask the same question—how is your team? What did you learn from these power coffee dates? The reply always leads to another conversation about how they can mentor someone into a bigger role or delegate more to lighten their own load. By giving your time and energy to your team you can empower them on a deep soul level to fast-track a company's roadmap to success and it's a win-win for everyone.

Here are three connection strategies you can use to power up your team and business partnerships to feel valued.

1. **Value your relationships.** When I ran TORSTAR, I made the twenty-four-hour-each-way trip to London every quarter to meet with a client, staying seventy-two hours to meet with our brand partners, host media events, and deliver market insights. Between those commitments I coffee-dated and caught up with friends. There was no time for jet lag, as I had to power up and be present to deliver the impact with each commitment. I always felt highly valued by one of our retail clients, as she was also a mum and without saying it in person, she knew the sacrifices I made to be available for international work commitments during the week and my daughter on the weekend. Upon arrival she nurtured me by booking our initial meeting time in a nail bar or foot massage before we got down to the nitty-gritty of results and delivery. I always wanted to go above and beyond for this client as she took the time to understand what it was like to be in my shoes.

2. **Create the time with a walk-and-talk strategy.** Look at the size of your team and you can become overwhelmed with how you

can create and invest personalized time to get to know them better. I get it and have been you. Nature is the biggest healer and creator of relationships and nothing is stopping you from sharing your morning walk or run with a team member. Break it down by committing to two walk-and-talks (or runs) per week then bring the team together for a bonding session a few months later. You will be surprised at what you learn from each other, and the conversations others are empowered to have outside of a normal "meeting" that bring the team together in a positive and rewarding way.

3. **Celebrate what matters.** Remembering birthdays and work anniversaries shows you are invested and care about the connection and partnership. A simple text, handwritten card, flowers, or gift is an action and acknowledgment this person means something to you.

These three strategies work, as when a person feels understood it builds trust, loyalty, and commitment in a relationship, placing you firmly in their tribe as a respected connection. Listening to others means you can better understand their perspectives, leading to more constructive conversations where you feel your point of view is being considered and validated. These are the people with whom you feel you can make magic happen. They're as fired up about your ideas as you are, and they dive into them fully, adding, taking on, and helping you bring them to life. What's not to love about that?

CHAPTER TWELVE

Stepping into Your Power Zone and Finding Your Purpose

"It is through the power of our story that we find our purpose."

—Tory Archbold

I t is liberating being in your power zone, as there is not a cloud in the sky and the sun is constantly shining. You wake up, the beat of your heart feels vibrant, and you glow from the inside out. You're in flow with life because you are seamlessly walking through doors meant for you and allowing others to walk through doors meant for them. You have created boundaries around what others can expect from you and you from them.

You can walk into any situation anywhere in the world at any time of day and enjoy the moment because you have mastered the art of being present. You operate at a high frequency, the level others want to lean into or aspire to step up and join. You become the teacher because you understand the law of dynamic exchange, which is unconditional and from the heart. The ultimate level of power anyone can have comes from within and starts with the art of happiness. This zone money cannot buy and comes from doing the inner work on *you* to unleash it. Are you ready to surrender to the process and become that person?

Many people live in their comfort bubbles. Why? Because it is so easy! But easy never challenges you to step up to the next level. If you're on cruise control, you are not stepping into your power, nor are you stepping into what you came here to achieve—transformation through the power of self-belief. Doing those things that make you feel uncomfortable; they are the magic moments. They raise your vibration, and they make you uniquely you. Let's test ourselves for a moment—if you had to write down on a piece of paper three things that scare you about a situation and challenge yourself to confront them, what would they be? Mine was saying goodbye to the old and hello to the new, online dating and removing people from my life who were not aligned with where I was heading. I had tough decisions and power moves to make and yes, I felt scared, vulnerable, and uneasy about how things may or may not work out. But when I embraced surrendering to the process, my life turned around in the most magical way. How about you? What's your truth? How do you want to shape your future? How will you raise your vibration? Most importantly, how will you step out of your own way and make this happen for *you*?

You may be rich with assets or surrounded by material wealth such as a Chanel handbag, a fabulous five-carat ring, and a pair of Jimmy Choos, but are you happy? A few years ago, I decided to put this to the test. We placed our plans on hold to move to the US: my daughter was in a toxic private school environment, the type where students spit on you if you weren't the flavor of the month, and she felt that was not OK and I agreed. It was two weeks into the school term, and we had planned to move in June. She simply refused to go back into that school environment. Who could blame her? I had to find a solution, and this is where the magic of miracles started appearing, as we could clearly see the magic of doors opening for us and doors being gently shut and left behind. We set an intention for what her next "educational" move would be and landed on two options. She could change schools in our area (which would be a simple uniform switch, not necessarily changing the school environment that seemed to be gaining momentum with competitive parents and kids lacking respect for themself and others) or remove herself from that environment and join a boarding community in the country, where life would be more structured and simpler. Each night while going through this process, we asked what the right outcome would be, and the answer was always the same—boarding school, which she loved.

For the first time in a long time, I was alone. My plans had not gone the way I intended: to move countries and start again, which was now not possible with a child in boarding school in another country than where I wanted to live. I had to surrender and simply set another intention. "What is meant to appear so I fully align with my destiny." I had done the inner work, cleared the deck, and had nothing to lose and everything to gain—it was the year of "love and adventure," and that's precisely when my husband appeared. The universe had ensured my daughter was in a safe environment she loved, and I was given the space to meet my soulmate and build a relationship with him within months. You might be asking what this has to do with being in your power zone. It's simple; I had a plan to shift my energy forward. I switched my thinking and did it differently, leasing out my four-bedroom home to downsize into a two-bedroom apartment, which started the process of stripping out old energy to bring in the new. I recognized my old life may not work with the new life, which meant sacrifice.

This decision started when I was dating my husband. He walked into a shit storm of old energy in a home cluttered with the past when he was my future. He no doubt thought I was a hoarder with all four-bedroom wardrobes stacked full of clothes, some with price tags on them and over sixty designer handbags I never used. Like many women in business, I had surrounded myself with material items to "look good" on the outside but had forgotten about the inside. I could not even use the excuse that I worked in fashion and had to look good; he wasn't buying into it and said the best way to deal with this move was to sort everything into piles—what I wanted to keep, what I wanted to give away, and what I wanted to dump. He was extremely patient with me when I said, "But maybe I can use this or wear this at some point"—um, no. If you haven't used it in the last six months, why do you need it? Men can be so black and white, and it was just the spiritual medicine I needed to hear.

The idea was for Bella and me to take two suitcases to the apartment and streamline our life for a year. We both struggled with leaving the luxury of space but what we learnt was the greatest gift in return. You don't need much to live a happy life. We wore the same clothes repeatedly and started to appreciate the simplicity because we weren't surrounded by an overload of "choice." When the time came to move back into our home a year later, we stripped what remained *again*. It felt liberating and we repeated the same process—what we wanted to keep, what we wanted to give away, and what we wanted to sell or dump. We had successfully removed the conditioned belief that you needed material items to prove your self-worth that had obscured our powerful selves.

I met a close friend for coffee a while ago and over our piccolos she said something that stuck with me: "Everything you used to talk about wanting in your life has found you." I listened. "Your business success. Your happy daughter. Your global connections. Your supportive husband. Your health and energy. The way you say you want something then work out how to get it inspires me." I want to make it clear this is not about how great my life is. It's about the power of manifesting whatever it is you want your life to look like, which means shifting your perspective to get clear on what you want. I wanted to share my life with a man I loved—how could I do that with no spare wardrobe for his clothes to hang? That meant creating the space for what I wanted and that was him.

I also shared with her these four powerful steps on how to build confidence when preparing your next power move into a zone of fulfillment and alignment.

1. **Look at the facts and take credit for your accomplishments.** Write them down and own them. It's the "feel good" factor of life.

2. **Follow people you feel are accomplished and aligned with your values, intent, and purpose**—you will learn a lot from them and their community by simply leaning in. Unfollow the ones that aren't aligned with how you wish to move forward.

3. **You don't need to be perfect;** in fact, making mistakes is an important step in learning and allows us to evolve as leaders, mothers, and partners. Some of my greatest mistakes have become my greatest achievements because they have empowered me to own the mistake and then step up and shine.

4. **The simple shifts in life are often the most powerful.** If you want to step up in the world, stop procrastinating and just start. Your plan may shift, just like mine—that's OK too. Be agile in your thinking and most importantly embrace the experience as a miracle may appear at the end.

Journalist and author Jacinta Tynan experienced the gift of new opportunities with a mindset shift, which landed her a dream role interviewing women on topics that light her up from the inside. While she's not diligent about committing to three coffee dates a week—preferring to drink tea—she finds it provides the perfect "cover" to reach out to others who she may not necessarily know or spend any time with, with no other agenda than to connect. Through joining our #CoffeeChallenge she found "a way we can support others in career or life" because she understood the power of a mutual exchange of energy. The more people she connected with, the more she realized we all have far more in common than we don't and found it "uplifting and empowering." For Jacinta, every coffee/tea date she has been on has led somewhere, whether it's a story idea, a refreshing new perspective, a collaboration, or a new friend. She generated her dream role by having the courage to reach out and connect with others simply by having the impetus to ask an editor to meet for coffee (even though she drank hot chocolate).

Jayne Williams, a certified nutritionist, believes stepping into your power zone means finding your purpose and truly "walking through it." Wisdom comes from action, doing the work, and walking through the other side, knowing you can't travel any other way than what you know you are called to do. She describes her journey as a bumpy road and "believes our mess is our message; our wounds are our beauty. Our story comes from taking the journey, getting lost, taking the wrong path, then taking the right one, almost giving up, surrendering, and then seeing the light through the darkness." That is when Jayne realized her purpose—empowering, teaching, and guiding others to get healthy and build a life they love, which required her to walk her own health journey to truly understand why that was her purpose. She took action to get out of her own way and figure out how she could help herself. "For me, it was an unlayering process. Past trauma, stubbornness, procrastination, lack of confidence were all reasons I told myself I couldn't do it. I needed to focus on simple steps to move toward understanding and appreciating my life, my body, to start to make changes that would help me move into my power."

Her turning point was attending an event where she was asked to write herself a letter. In the letter, she was told to write down accomplishments on how she had impacted others' lives. It was the first time she had stopped and written down an "impact list" and received the letter in the mail six months later, opened it, and cried. The miracle was Jayne received it at a time she was feeling stuck on the next step. As she read the letter based on comments, testimonials, opportunities, speaking engagements, successful programs, and partnership opportunities she had dreamed about coming true, she knew she was doing what she should be doing, working with entrepreneurs and health and wellness practitioners to unlayer pain points and realize their gifts. "When that happens, you can see in their eyes, their action, their words, their being, they are ready to take off. It's this fearless, powerful stance that creates a foundation for what they want their impact to look like. Since that letter, I have not looked back, only forward!"

Write a Letter to Yourself Here

Erika Cramer is often referred to as the Cardi B of the personal development world, as she is a survivor of childhood abuse, has been in and out of the foster care system, and found herself in a confronting car accident that killed her fiancé and gave her life. She takes ownership of everything in her life. When you speak with her, nothing is off-record; it is as it is. That's the beauty of Erika—she speaks her truth from deep within her soul, like the women I choose to stand alongside in life. She found her purpose through her entangled life, like many women who have those breakthrough moments, simply because they put their hands up and said, *"Enough, I am ready to embrace change; show me the signs and I will do what needs to be done!"*

Erika is Puerto Rican via Boston in the United States. When she arrived in Australia, she worked with a coach who forced her to look in the mirror and realize, "The common denominator of all the hot mess of my life was *me!*" She had been in multiple terrible relationships (sound familiar?) and deep trauma she was unaware of was hidden because she didn't know what it meant to work on herself. A guy she had been seeing broke up with her on her birthday and she thought, "WTF is going on here? This must have something to do with me; what can I do?" A typical people-pleasing trait. Her personal trainer suggested she work with someone to confront what was holding her back and she said, "I'm so done with this all, let's do this; let's go." She started seeing a life coach who helped unravel her life story and trauma; she was excited about the opportunity presented amongst the mess. "I had been through so much pain and trauma. It was so terrible, and yet, here I was, finding all these opportunities and gaining so much from unpacking pain and taking responsibility for it. This process got me so excited about going on a journey of self-discovery, working on self, it got me fired up and wanting to commit to doing the self-work."

Through this process Erika recognized, "Everything that happened to me *had happened for me*," and in doing the inner work, "realized there were so many other women out there just like me. Women whose past were holding them back from going for what they want or whose past had become the catalyst for going for exactly what they wanted." She cracked her "life code," which was showing other women why they are resilient, why they overcome adversity, and how they could show up and do the work to create the life they ultimately want. At that moment her powerful business was born as she recognized her purpose.

Erika entered that power zone by "working on my shit. Dealing with challenges. Unpacking all that had happened and finding myself. My pain was my up level, the answers of who I am and what I need to do in the world. I found wisdom in my pain. I went into it, faced it, went head-on into the dark night of the soul. I paid for help even when I didn't have the money for it. I put it on credit cards, I did the hard yards. I excavated the platinum and the gold that was hiding in the shit of my life. It was shit, but in that shit there were all these hidden treasures I would have missed if I wasn't committed to working on myself."

We often face fear during this transformational process with negative thought processes, such as, "How am I going to pay for this?" and "What will people think?" I get it because I have been that person. Burnt out with everything holding me back, I decided to take a leap of faith and say yes to my future. During this process I was afraid that if I invested in myself by reducing the hours I was available to work, I couldn't pay the school fees that gave my daughter the structure in life she needed to power her up. The opposite happened. People were prepared to pay more to secure my time and I attracted an even higher caliber of client into my orbit. How did I do it? I reframed my thinking.

Reframing your thinking with a powerful "what if" exercise will empower you to switch your thinking and view the challenge you face as a possibility.

What if...

- **I went without a night out with friends for a one-hour session with a mentor or attended an event tapping into the power of others to up-level my life?**

- **I got up an hour early to write in my journal and get clear on my goals to find a more innovative way to achieve them?**

- **I said no to the friend who drained me and invested more time in the friend who inspired me?**

- **I sold some items in my wardrobe or home that are collecting dust to pay for something that would uplevel my life and better serve someone else?**

- **And so on...**

When I let go of the fear and said, "I am doing this; why should I hold myself back?" it felt liberating, and it was a step toward my power zone. My daughter was in year six, I was downsizing my business, and there was no love on the horizon. I had nothing to lose and everything to gain. I don't know about you, but I found it hard at that struggle point in my life to ask for help as everyone always saw me as a strong, successful, independent woman. In hindsight, their expectation was that I was that woman who didn't need help. I now recognize I was not alone in that thought process, as asking for help often makes people feel uneasy because it requires surrendering control to someone else. Another fear when asking for help is a perception of being perceived as needy—nobody wants to feel ashamed of their situation or come across as incompetent. I now understand the power of asking for help shifts energy forward and is to be celebrated, not feared, regardless of whether the answer is a yes or no. The outcome is always determined by your mindset and how you **choose** to propel forward. By asking for help, I chose to embrace change and it fast-tracked my transformation.

When you are ready to surrender, the right people come into your life as you trust your intuition and follow the signs. One of the self-investments I wanted to make was self-care and leaning into the energy blocks I had to conquer to move forward. I had been looking for retreats that offered a platform for nurturing and growth. I came across a retreat hosted at The Ranch in Malibu by the rockstar Shaman, Alyson Charles. I was hooked on the power of her narrative and the possibilities she offered. *Forbes* names her "a leading Shaman for expanding others into their full gifts and power." The *Huffington Post* championed her as "a top limit-breaking female founder." *Dazed* magazine named her "one of the top seven wellness accounts on Instagram," and *Marie Claire* magazine selected her as a cover story and "the next big thing."

Powerful stories speak to me as I find they always unearth something inside that looks at life through a different lens. Alyson's story was powerful—she went from being a national champion athlete, top-rated radio host, and national daytime television talk show host to aligning with her calling as a Shaman after a traumatic moment provided her awakening. She had done a backflip in life through success and survival and her willingness to share her experience with others spoke to me as it was empowering and inspirational. The retreat she promoted was about bringing in your life mission for the year ahead and I felt called to go. One slight problem—the dates didn't work as my daughter was returning to school and I wanted to be there and support that process, so I signed up for her newsletter and received an email about an opening to work one-on-one with her after the retreat. My heart said yes, and it was one of the most transformational experiences I have invested in as she unleashed my power from within simply by sharing hers.

Alyson began to consciously align with her calling around 2012, when she experienced a simultaneous Divine intervention, guiding her to face her greatest fears. Walking through those fears, she could release denial and illusions that had deeply plagued her life experience. Through this soul-awakening and miracle intervention, three key steps revealed her next powerful move and she explained it like this:

1. I was not who I thought I was and I needed to finally get out of my own way and allow support. I achieved this through surrendering. I spoke to my soul, great spirit, and great Mother Earth and asked to be shown the way.

2. I took responsibility and heeded the guidance and instructions that immediately poured in. In my devotion to facing myself and healing,

the always-present ancient wisdom within me finally had space to open more.

3.   I finally allowed myself to be consciously aware of what these deep wisdom truths wanted to share.

Ever since her awakening, Alyson has lived in direct spiritual alignment and followed the instructions that the vertical line of connection provides. The three connection points in the steps she took have guided and shown her the next step her soul needs to evolve in, the next aspect/shadow component she needs to face and transcend within, and the next vision provided to reveal the way she can be of service with her Shamanic and spiritual gifts. Alyson believes deeply in this guidance system that is deep within us all as it "always guides me in embodying even greater love, wholeness, integrity, conscious awareness so that I find even more of myself and my Divine power every day." She explains it as an infinite evolutionary process that carries huge magic and miracles, and at times intense initiations and fires, that allow you to embrace your human self.

Throughout her life journey, Alyson trusted herself to follow the signs and recognized when birthing an idea was simply the wrong timing. She became agile in her thinking, like when she was asked to write her first book, thought the timing was right, and flew to Bali to begin writing. During her morning meditation, power animals as far as her mind's eye could see entered, asking that she shelve that original book idea (which ironically was a book on the art of surrender) and co-create a modern-day power animal guidebook with them.

In her own words, "to arrive at a point in my relationship with the power animal guides where they trusted me to be a voice for them was deeply moving as I have always trusted them to show up on-demand when I'm on stage in front of audiences of over 10,000 doing live power animal readings. I bravely surrendered and steadfastly held a very clear, strong line for what I knew and was instructed that this book should be in terms of the energetic medicine it embodies, the Shamanic wisdom and education held within it, the art that each of the hundred animals must accurately portray their healing attributes and wisdoms to a greater world. It was the biggest and most arduous task of my career, but I could not be happier as the *Animal Power* book is now a bestseller."

I don't often cry; the last time was at my wedding because I was so happy to come into alignment with the family I always wanted and dreamed of. I asked Alyson about the standout moment she had that helped another birth their own gift. I am sharing her response for you. If you question whether you can step into your power zone, don't. You can and you will. You will hear a calling deep inside of you to step up and into your power, so don't ignore it. When you become willing to step up and into the vibration of your life calling to transcend to the next level, anything is possible in this lifetime. All it takes is self-belief and a powerful step forward to say yes to yourself and yes to transformation. Through the power of reading others' stories throughout this book, you can see that life can be a beautiful hot mess and none of us are alone on the highway of life, if we are willing to ask for help. You should also see that you are the only one that can turn that hot mess into your powerful success story by simply answering your calling to step up and into your power to serve others in your unique way.

This is Alyson's response and I share it with deep gratitude in my heart: "There are countless examples of clients who finally tapped into their own power to leave dysfunctional relationships, toxic workplaces, move across the world simply because they had learnt to hear the 'calls' of the Divine (and soul), and it directed them there, so that they could learn to trust their intuition and launch huge businesses and charitable organizations etc. But my time with you [Tory] comes to the forefront of my mind! Working with you could honestly be the example of what an ideal 'student' or 'client'/Shaman dynamic is. You were unwavering in your willingness to grow, to expand in your spiritual truth and calling, to do any and all work and practices required to get you into even clearer and stronger alignment with your new path, and there was simply nothing that could stop you or your soul's knowing that this new way must be born and shared with the world. You took responsibility, faced what needed to be faced, and you were, and continue to be, on fire in your ability to let the new that needs to be born through you, happen! To witness you pivot from such a massive previous self-built career to shifting into a place where you can truly be of service for others and assist them in not just alleviating their suffering but also truly step into the soul-aligned work they incarnated here to be of service with, is astoundingly beautiful to watch."

Amen to that, and A'ho to Alyson, who empowered me to find my calling and birth it. Now it's over to you to back yourself to do the same.

Total Alignment

*"Remove what no longer serves you
to find peace with what does."*

—Tory Archbold

What does alignment actually mean? It's using your unique talents and aligning them with your personal mission and professional ambitions by surrendering to what you know and feel you are meant to be doing in this lifetime by feeling a deep connection to what you are creating each day as a partner, sibling, friend, and leader. Total alignment means consistently showing up as the person you know you are. It means speaking your truth, living your values, and being a person of integrity. **When we own our story, we own our power—life is that simple.** Through sharing the power of our story and the story of others we can tap into a resource that stimulates our thought process and life choices. Remember, we are never alone when we face a challenge as someone has walked that same road searching for the answers you are now seeking many times before. Tapping into the power of how others translated challenges into possibilities gives us permission to dig deep and action a solution when the timing feels right. Throughout the years, listening or reading the stories of others has given me many aha moments, which empowered me to shift my thinking and move my story forward. I call these "game-changing moments," and they are why I am with you today, paying my knowledge forward so you can reach for the stars too.

The opportunity to work in flow and become an unstoppable force of attraction comes through the power of self-belief. Yes, we absolutely can do this. "Yes" because opportunity surrounds everyone and is available to claim and honor when you choose to take a powerful step forward and shift energy in your favor—that is how you will begin to see "flow" in your life experiences and know that you are on track to wake up with a happy heart and attract those miracles waiting for you. I use the word "honor," as the best advice a mentor gave was to remain grounded and humble when life's gifts appear. Honor this blessing because "you will become a conduit and vessel for change," meaning we are given this portal to lift up others, our teams, our communities, and the vibration of everything that we encounter with daily and consistent gratitude from the heart. When you recognize you are the "conduit or vessel" you will also recognize this is a gift you have been given to lead and enable change. As soon as you dip into "ego" or "this is mine, look at me" territory, your vessel will sink as it's a sign you are out of alignment with your purpose and not living a life anchored to your values. I believe that anyone on earth can be a conduit; there is nothing stopping you from claiming that crown and coming into alignment with who you are meant to become—you just need to face your greatest fears.

If you are fearful about how alignment looks for you ask for help or simply shift your focus into a more positive mindset by journaling and mapping out the framework of that next-level version of you. There is a saying attributed to Buddha Siddhartha Gautama Shakyamuni and the Theosophists that "when the student is ready, the teacher will appear." Be prepared to do the soul work, manifest, and lean into the power of community, because dreams come true when you decide the path you wish to take. You may have noticed small shifts in your everyday life already supporting your journey to align with your truth. That transformational breakthrough you are looking for is heading your way—feel it and see it!

Five Signposts to Build Momentum and Embrace Change

Every time this happens in your life, give yourself a silent nod of gratitude and thanks for your progress. It's a way to tip the universe and acknowledge how far you have come.

1. **You frequently see number sequences** or angel numbers like 1111, 2222, 444, 333, and 555. I started seeing those in Kyoto years ago, and that was the start of my journey. Today I can read sequences of numbers that deliver messages and show the lessons I still need to learn or affirm I am on track. For instance, 1111 means it's time to connect with your intuition. 1234 means you're on the right

SELF-BELIEF IS YOUR SUPERPOWER

track in life—an incredibly powerful sign I wish for everyone around the world to see!

2. **You start to feel more energetically supported**—you don't lean into toxic friendships, family connections, and work colleagues anymore—your tribe radiates a positive, happy vibe that delivers immense joy and inner peace. You may even sleep better at night!

3. **Your intuition has kicked in and inspiring ideas start flowing in that you know you want to activate.** This might be to move into a role that suits your passion and purpose. You may create and develop a new business idea or take that three-month trip overseas to honor you. Whatever your idea, you want to activate it and live in flow.

4. **Your journaling has empowered you to manifest** not one *big* idea but a ton of small things at once through your commitment to the morning shower ritual. What you wanted is finding its way to you because you have shifted your mindset through the power of surrender.

5. **Things keep working out for you even when faced with unexpected challenges** as you now lean into the power of viewing challenges as possibilities. You know that challenge is a lesson and a nudge to level up your thinking and honor your role in making the world a better place.

Look at What Inspires You to Seek Answers

When I was running TORSTAR my inspiration for global retail was born from the fact that I loved traveling and understanding what consumer trends delivered impact in the world. The brands we represented also loved understanding the experience customers enjoyed from the point of engagement with their brand to the point of possession or purchase. I often watched this process as I browsed in some of the most incredible retail malls in the world, going from shop to shop, learning how staff would treat and nurture others on their customer journey. I found it fascinating and could see why some brands were successful where others failed. When online shopping came into play, I would always encourage clients to invest in the brand experiences of others and order from them online to understand how products were delivered in terms of packaging, personalized notes, additional offers, and follow-ups, which they would outsource to our team. Again, I would sit back and watch these items being unwrapped and what delivered impact versus what was cast aside if it was considered a "blah" effort from the brand. It became crystal clear brand leaders were leaders because of the community they chose to be part of. Suzy Menkes, then fashion editor of the international *New York Times*, understood that and started hosting luxury fashion conferences to bring the fashion community together to share the power of their stories and allow the industry to learn, grow, and evolve. I attended conferences in Berlin, London, and Singapore, listening to the power of the relationships she had built with the likes of Karl Lagerfeld, Ermenegildo Zegna, the Missoni family, Frida Giovanni (my favorite female speaker and ex–creative director at Gucci),

Victoria Beckham, and HRH Princess Marie-Chantal. Suzy's little black book of connections was diverse and fascinating. She attracted the best of the best and I loved leaning into the power of their story and how they built their brands. It inspired me to lead the brands and teams we partnered with to the next level of success by thinking creatively about customer journeys and global advocacy to secure the merger and acquisition deals they were after.

At the Singaporean conference, my path crossed with Gina de Vee, a women's empowerment coach and creator of Divine Living in the United States. She mentored Jen Sincero, bestselling author, speaker, and self-confessed cattle prod. I call it a Divine intervention for us, as she was not from the fashion set yet understood the power of expanding your mindset by leaning into the wisdom of others. I asked her why she was there, and she said she wanted to start a fashion label. I remember questioning *why* when she was clearly so good at what she did—empowering women to build successful businesses on their own terms—and advised her not to take that path. Her advice to me? Strip out the toxic people in your life so you come into alignment with your destiny. We were brutally honest with each other and built a friendship I value and trust that involves leaning into each other for advice or a laugh when we hit those pivotal life moments and go, "Argggggghhhhh, what's next?!" I always say find a friend who loves you unconditionally as they are a friend for life. That's who Gina is to me.

Gina describes finding her purpose when she aligned with her truth. This alignment came when she was reading the true and ancient story of Queen Esther of Persia. She had read it many times before, but this time, it leapt off the page and was no longer just about her story. "I saw my own story in it. I knew that what's most personal is most universal. I really dived in and studied that, started looking at that body of work in an entirely different way so that I could bring it out into the world." One of modern times' misconceptions is that we're taught to go out, get, and do, make it happen, and figure it out, yet sometimes it is just waiting for you in the wings of life if you dare to look.

We also need to value what brings us into alignment by recognizing what takes us off-piste. In essence, this means understanding our trigger points, which is our ability to feel, express, and manage a range of positive and negative emotions to form and maintain good relationships with others. I have always worked in the business of people, connection, and engagement. My role is to fill other people's cups so they can build successful life stories professionally and personally. How can I do that with a half-empty cup? I can't, which means I must be firm with boundary creation, so I don't take on others' negative energies or emotions or place myself in a situation of overwhelm. Think of it like this—what lights you up and keeps you on a path in the direction of positively fulfilling your dreams versus what decisions you are making that take you off-piste.

It's simple to work out what alignment feels like for you as in your five-point story you would have recognized the patterns you needed to break and the life moments that light you up. Take a moment to reshare them with yourself and then make the time to commit to ensure those moments that lit you up happen more often as that's a clear directive to the universe that you want to live a life in alignment with your truth. If you keep seeing repetitive, bad energetic patterns, you are off-piste and the work you need to do starts now as you are yet to own your truth.

To kick off your thoughts process, this is what lights me up:

- **Once or twice a year take time out for self-care in a retreat.** I do this because I need a "me moment" when I am not accountable to anyone but myself. I do this to quiet my mind, body, and spirit because I recognize I need to give back to myself to become whole again.

- **Road trips with my daughter deliver a sense of freedom.** We open the sunroof, sing songs from the '80s and '90s at full blast and fall into deep conversation about life. I cherish these moments and they make me happy.

- **My daily morning walk-and-talk with my husband.** This is our time together to lean into each other (outside the bedroom), be in nature, and workshop ideas or visions we both have and want to bring to life.

- **Travel to far-flung destinations and the discovery of new cultures.** This keeps me alive, and thankfully I married a man who loves this as much as my daughter. We never sit still in one country for long, as we have a thirst for new and exciting experiences.

- **Dinner parties at home.** While I cannot cook, I value my friends and the conversation they bring to the table. Their laughter energizes me along with the crazy dancing and power chats at the end of the night.

I know that these five moments I cherish and invest in my life will always flow. What moments light you up?

In business we can also come unstuck or be presented with opportunities that don't feel aligned with our future. While going through the process of selling TORSTAR, accepting millions of dollars felt "off-piste" to me as the buyers didn't seem like an energy match. "Here's the down payment, now go and deliver attitude," which works for some people, but it didn't work for me as I believed in teamwork and the power of partnership to attract and create. My business was built on love. We attracted those brands and people because of our value set—our passion, integrity, and delivery to become the best of the best for those we represented. The business model I had created was not about chasing dollars, it was about what we could create to make a difference. Selling a business to chase or receive a dollar seemed shallow and out of alignment with where I was headed. I gently pulled back as I knew the millions they offered would find me in other ways if I trusted the process. That decision was made because I knew the power of surrendering to what felt right, and I also understood the power that something bigger would present itself when the timing was right. Yes, you may be thinking that's a tough call to make, but I believe in the power of Divine timing and life lessons. I never questioned the process; I felt and leaned into it.

Why Your Ego Lands Nowhere Special

I've watched women get to the 80 percent mark in their careers. They aggressively want and target the next 20 percent, a CEO or prestigious board role, and they keep losing the opportunity because their ego gets in the way. They want it so badly yet are afraid to face the reality of why their ego is failing them in the quest to obtain their career goals. These women never find alignment because they do not know how to find themselves. They are completely focused on work, driven by the dollar, title accolade, and the material wealth they can display and cut others down because they want to remain in control. The truth of the pattern is this—the universe will always come along and slap them down a notch by firing them from the role, forcing them to resign or accept a redundancy, creating much-needed time for them to invest in themselves, dig deep, and truly understand who they are and what they want from life so that they learn the lesson and level up again. It's a game of choice, and while some choose to learn, some choose never to learn, which is why the same lesson repeats itself. These women will never glow from the inside or reach the stars they so desperately want to touch because they are unbalanced and out of alignment with their truth. They do not like what they see in the mirror and likely lack self-love. If you can relate, the biggest gift you can give yourself in these situations is the gift of time by learning to love who you see in the mirror. Chase your next goal when you have faced your truth as that is where you can grow and stand in your power. No title or bad attitude toward others will ever give you the CEO crown because they live in ego, not heart.

On the other spectrum, evolved women face their truth. They might fear that truth, but they make time to face and own it. When Gina realized her business life was out of alignment, she described it as, "When you wake up and realize you're falling out of love with a person. I was falling out of love and was afraid of change because that was how I created my identity, how I created my money." She kept thinking she needed to work harder, get the numbers up or face the hard truth and change something from within. As she says, "When you don't listen and trust what your actual desires are, you're going to be miserable." The turning point was when her father went into the hospital unexpectedly. She was at his bedside, not knowing if he would live or die. In that confronting moment, she decided to surrender and allow the universe to bring her back into alignment. "I let go of how I know how to make money, who I think I am, my identity taking the courageous leap to close 90 percent of my business. I didn't know what I was going to do next, and it took a full year of living in a world in between worlds to receive the answer." Through this process of surrender, Gina found her truth and reignited her passion, allowing her to skyrocket her business to the next level. She focused on femininity and spirituality through her book *The Audacity to Be Queen* and a podcast, app, and program called *Own Your Throne*. She could do this because she let go of ego and owned the power of who she was.

Become Unbreakable by Understanding the Power of Your Truth

I sat down with Jay Glazer, an American TV personality who, after years of rejection, built a career as one of the most iconic sports insiders, which earnt him a spot on the Emmy-winning *Fox NFL Sunday* and a role as himself alongside Dwayne "The Rock" Johnson on HBO series *Ballers*. When asked what aligned him with his life purpose, his answer was simple: "It began with me being broken and now I'm unbreakable." Jay understood what it's like to be broken, struggle, and be rejected more than anybody else. He started his career making $9,750 a year living in New York City, out-working everybody, not by a little, but by a lot. If they worked forty hours a week, he would work a hundred. He didn't accept money from anybody; he did it himself, as he believed in creating and stepping into his own destiny. Jay became the first minute-by-minute breaking newscaster, covering football in America and becoming a host on the number one television show in America. He thought making it to the top of his game would be "rainbows and unicorns," but instead discovered "if you don't know how to love yourself from the inside out, all that stuff you're trying to get from the outside in, it doesn't fulfill you like we think it does. You see it in movies, and you see it on TV shows, so you think that's what happens, but it's not really what happens."

A game-changing near-death experience changed his life. He needed the wake-up call as he kept prioritizing work and ignoring the advice of medical staff surrounding him. This experience came at him hard and fast so when a hospital room began to visually move away from him. He put his phone down, realized he was in trouble, and said, "Uh-oh. God, I think I'm coming to see you. And if I am, it's OK and I love you. But I still think there's more to do here in this world. If you save me, I promise you I'll do bigger things in this world and make a difference." You and I know people around the world make that deal with God all the time, but once they get better, they forget it. His wish was granted as his oxygen went from seventy-six to ninety-three with no medical explanation. Jay knows why—it was to birth his next powerful journey as a conduit by standing in his truth.

He opened his first business focusing on mindset switches and named it "Unbreakable" because his experiences didn't break him; they made him. In his words, "Whatever breaks you, you can come through the other side of the tunnel; you can use that as strength anywhere." He then tapped into his life experience to create a charity inside his Unbreakable Hollywood gym where he coached combat veterans and ex-athletes to inspire them to step into their own personal power, reframing their minds, bodies, and souls. Next, he wrote a bestselling book, where he bravely stood in his truth and spoke about what was going on in his life to encourage others to face their mental demons.

What Jay feared most became his greatest asset as he chose to remove a fear of judgment to speak his truth. He suffered from a deep, dark depression on the inside while the outside world saw him as a sports hero. He didn't believe the two worlds could merge. When depression hit him in the past, he "used to just pop Vicodin, have a bunch of booze, go out there and be the life of the party—I was fake." Now he has the strength to say, "I can't go out tonight," and when his friends ask, "Why?" he says, "The beast just got out of the box and it's kicking my ass today." Jay learnt the power of stepping up by leaning into his "team" of friends and professionals to acknowledge what was going on in his life and it gave him alignment. "Every one of my friends are the baddest motherfuckers on the planet. Every one of them I've opened up to about this, it has brought us so much closer together. No one's going to call you a wuss. No one's going to tell you to suck it up. So that's why I'm out there sharing my story to show people that you can lean into people and then they will admire you for this strength."

Honesty was a power move for Jay because, when he was on camera at times, he felt like he was having a heart attack, which was a panic attack, yet he told no one through fear of judgment. His hands would shake and he would sweat, eyes darting back and forth. "I start getting very labored in my breath, my heart started racing and it happened every single time I ever went on air and became habitual. It just came on and then it continued. The world didn't talk about panic attacks, anxiety attacks and mental health until twelve years after this happened to me. So, for those twelve years I was getting my heart checked out for a heart attack. I didn't know any better. All that time I thought I was having a heart attack—that should've given me a heart attack!" He learnt what got him through these panic attacks was laughter and acceptance. "If you watch me crack early on in our show, if I start with a really corny joke, a bad joke, a joke that doesn't fit, it's really just to get me through a panic attack." Jay owned his truth and life experiences to speak out and empower others as "knew I had the power to help." He told me that self-care is OK and necessary. "I've learnt it's OK to slow down, people won't forget you and they are rooting for you to take time for yourself." Now that's alignment from the inside out and he continually pays it forward by "checking" in on his teammates too.

Break through Barriers and Stand in Your Power

I met Vanessa Bell during lockdown and a Zoom coffee date. She was on a remote property in NSW, and I was in Sydney—we both dressed up because that's who we are when we commit to connecting with someone special. In her twenties, Vanessa travelled the world as an international model and has had some extraordinary life experiences. She married a farmer and became one of the only women in the world with a major landholding more than twice the size of Paris. The true power of her story was born from acceptance when she went partially blind in her left eye during a stressful period in her life when she experienced trauma and betrayal with an ex-partner. Going blind was the turning point for her to re-evaluate, take responsibility, and adopt a new mindset to charge forward in new and exciting ways to advocate for others on a global stage.

For years she was worried about what others might think of her actual "gift," which was heightened by living in small rural communities where people tend to lean into the gossip of the land. She learnt through the power of owning her story and standing in her truth that she could break through this barrier and live in alignment through acceptance of who she is and what she stands for. The gift of clarity came to Vanessa in two ways: via the healing power of yarn (knitting) and her ability to deliver profound messages to deliver a winning mindset through intuitive readings.

SELF-BELIEF IS YOUR SUPERPOWER

She recently found herself on the number-one breakfast radio show with Kyle and Jackie O (you're probably thinking, "What a coincidence"; I am thinking, "What incredible synchronicity!") and her reading for Kyle stopped traffic. It also showed her a new way of looking at how she could add value for others, which started with her ability to value herself. She started ramping up her actionable steps to make her wildest business dreams reality by transitioning from observing nature to observing herself. She committed to change and transformation through the power of what is being taught in this book. She harnessed the power of attracting what you deserve by committing to three coffee dates a week and built out a powerful digital footprint to attract the right opportunities one of which was to create a 100 percent Australian merino wool knitwear collection with a team she greatly admired. Her vision was to collaborate with someone who had worked within Victoria Beckham's design team, which she made a reality through the power of connection and not being afraid to ask for help.

Author, actress, and Yogi Rachel Coopes describes this process perfectly: "As we navigate life and try different things, we often feel like that disastrous relationship, job, or chapter was an utter waste of time, as it showed us who we are *not*, and what we *don't* want. It's only through butting our heads against what is not our purpose that we discover who and what we are and why we are here. It is through the process of making mistakes, that we move toward ultimately what we should be doing. And everyone's journey to that place will look and feel very different." The moral of any story is this. There is always a lesson to be learnt. There is always a powerful step to take to get to the destination and there is always someone, somewhere in the world that can help you make that happen. All you need to do is ask for help.

CHAPTER FOURTEEN

Your Next Powerful Step

"A happy heart is a magnet for miracles."

—Tory Archbold

The power of our story and the direction we choose to take in life does not end when you complete this book. We have a choice to move forward in a way that works for us, and choice is a powerful tool on the highway of life. Through leaning into the power of the stories shared you may feel a higher sense of purpose in your life, like you've been guided to level up and switch your thinking. Some chapters may have triggered new thought processes. It's all OK. A trigger means you're ready to face your truth and level up. Know that you are in the right place and on the right path as with self-belief you can achieve anything. It's a spiritual confirmation knowing you can, because you are coming into alignment with your highest self and understand the power of manifesting when you surrender to the process and trust yourself to follow the signs gifted to you.

When I need a reminder of the secret nudges of the universe all I do is reach out to people for a coffee date as it always opens me up to the power of thinking differently, of understanding where I can add value, or where I can further learn, grow, and evolve. The investment in coffee dates is not to be underestimated, as it will build a powerful network of opportunity where you can step up and make a difference by creating a movement that changes the lives of others in a business you may lead or an idea you wish to birth. The power of your investment in others is to be cherished, valued, and always anchored to your truth. Each connection you make brings you closer to making a difference because if you believe you can, you will. Trust the process because the process will trust you. You will find flow because you understand the power of surrender means the miracles of life appear when you need them most and often, they will appear in the most magical ways to teach you a lesson or show you how to move forward.

An example of flow happened recently when I went to New Zealand with my husband, and I believe it is because we both have happy hearts. We had no plans for a Saturday night out when we flew in. We saw a billboard for a Billy Joel concert and booked tickets, as it was his farewell tour and saw it as an opportunity to experience our first outdoor concert together. We got to the entry gates and our tickets were rejected by the scanner—turns out we had been scammed and the concert was 100 percent sold out. We went to the box office to explain the situation and, as I was standing there, this man who happened to play for the NZ Warriors said out of the blue, "You just need to surrender to the situation." We were 100 percent aligned with his thinking—maybe it was not meant to be. Less than thirty seconds later, a lady walked up and said, "I have two corporate tickets to give away as our friends didn't show up; does anybody want them?" Thank you, universe, and the lesson learnt was this: Billy Joel is a multi-

Grammy award–winning man who was seventy-three years old and still leaning into his passion for music. This passion came through the power of storytelling and one of his most famous quotes is this "if you're not doing what you love, you are wasting your time." In the seventh decade of his life, he was giving it his all and showing us all what to live for—passion, integrity, and people. He is a great example of a man who never gave up and is still pursuing his dreams because age is just a number. And, crazy as it sounds, that man from the NZ Warriors, whom we had never met before, walked past us twice on our morning coffee run in Sydney a month later. A reminder to always be deeply grateful for the unexpected gifts that find you along the highway of life.

I will share one more powerful story to ensure you recognize that nothing is ever beyond our reach. Dr. Jo Brown is an Australian who has spent twenty years committed to high-performance sports and championed champions as a sports physiotherapist working with over sixteen different sports at the international level. Her dream was to become an Olympic mindset coach. We met during lockdown—she had *big* goals that she wanted to make reality and committed to a series of our programs and one-on-one mentoring. One of those goals was to partner with global elite athletes and play a role in their Olympic journey. Three years later that dream and goal became reality. She believes high performance is a series of choices and requires taking a diagnostic look at performance (that is to "face it, you can fix it and forever fly"). This methodology has created partnerships with the Jamaican bobsled team (which qualified for the Beijing Olympics) and more recently US track star Noah Lyles. She has a happy heart because she worked on herself from the inside out, which has ultimately become her superpower, enabling her to partner with the world's best because she adds *value* to their dreams and ambitions.

The good news is you have now invested in your evolution by owning the power of your story. Through this process you will have become more aware of thoughts, feelings, beliefs, and opinions and will not be afraid to acknowledge and express who you are. Free of judgment, you can be you, on your own terms and at your own pace.

1. **You know who you are.**

2. **You know what you want.**

3. **You are in control of your destiny.**

4. **You surround yourself with the right people.**

5. **You don't compare yourself to others.**

6. **You do things every day to create the future you desire.**

7. **You notice the truth hidden in everything.**

8. **You want the best for yourself and others.**

So where to from here? Live every day like it's your last. Cherish the moment and don't be held back by what happened yesterday, the day before, the week before, the year before, or even decades ago. Stop complaining about your problems and work on them instead. Don't think about the things you can't change. Focus on the things you can act on and create your own opportunities. Be proactive. Stop waiting for others around you to do something and act—don't die with regrets; die knowing you did your best and your happy heart was a magnet for miracles. Commit to your growth—self-reflect, build on your strengths, and conquer your weaknesses. You are here because you can dream big and make that dream reality. And remember, a small step is a powerful step, and nothing is beyond your reach.

Much love, Tory xoxo

Offer Pages

Corporate Workshops

Want to bring the power of inspiration, advocacy, and growth to your organization? Powerful Steps regularly hosts formal trainings for team, organizations, and events. Check out **powerful-steps.com/mentor-global-entrepreneur-program/empowering-corporate.**

Learn how to understand the power of your personal brand, be visible in a virtual world, and build a strategy that attracts the type of clients you deserve.

For more information or to watch videos from my previous workshops, visit: **www.powerful-steps.com/speaking.**

I look forward to meeting you!

Digital Bonuses

We have so many wonderful bonuses for you along with this book, including:

◊ Self-Belief Mantras to support your daily journey (print-friendly)

◊ Discussion Questions for your book club or reading partner

◊ Morning Shower Ritual Video + Worksheet (This is my secret sauce to success!)

◊ Coffee Date Lesson + Worksheet: The Most Powerful Business Tool

To get your extra reader gifts, visit: **selfbeliefisyoursuperpower. com/bonus.**

Want to learn even more? We have curated the most helpful ways to advance your skills!

Network Like a
Pro Masterclass

Your Network Is Your Net Worth

Fast track your success by learning how to:

1. Convert coffee dates into clients

2. Focus on what matters most—you, your brand, and your message

3. Communicate with others with the true voice of a brand

4. Unlock the mystery of attracting your dream client

5. Build a community that adds to your bottom line

6. Stay grounded and humble while your star shines bright

This powerful masterclass will help you lead with impact and elevate the way the world sees you, no matter your age, career, or background.

Interested? Check out **classes.powerful-steps.com/courses/ network-like-a-pro**.

Business Attraction Program

Are you ready to own your story and unleash your power?

Learn to:

◊ Become a powerful leader, entrepreneur, or corporate warrior

◊ Step outside your comfort zone and into your power zone

◊ Become visible in a virtual world and attract what you deserve

◊ Build a powerful personal brand and digital footprint... the type where people call you!

This eight-week virtual training will help you step into your power, become a super attractor, and build your global tribe. Check out **powerful-steps. com/business-attraction-program** for more information.

Check out all of our Powerful Classes at: **powerful-steps.com/classes**.

Acknowledgments

This book was created through the power of connection, intuition, and, you guessed it: a coffee date. I have always trusted the magic of new beginnings. When something is meant to be, everything that is meant to support you falls perfectly into position and your A-Team is there to help you make it happen.

It is with deep gratitude that I say thank you to publishing powerhouse Lou Johnson for saying yes to a coffee date at Bills in Bondi on 16 January 2022. I knew she was the one to make my dream reality after seeing her on a global book tour which landed her in Miami taking on a role at Mango Publishing. She understood strategy and, most importantly, during that coffee date, she understood *me*. Author and journalist Jacinta Tynan had been encouraging me for many years to write a book, and I acknowledge her in my opening cheer squad of thank you's because without the right people by your side to support and consistently nudge you to make things happen, often you don't.

Without owning the power of our own story, we cannot shine a light for others. Not only does it give us a sense of freedom in our heart, it releases our fear of judgment and the unknown. Thank you to everyone who owned their story and shared it on the *Powerful Stories Podcast* and through a series of interviews for this book. You have given others a gift which is priceless, and I am truly grateful for you.

Thank you to Tina Clark for the introduction to Sarah Harden, CEO of Hello Sunshine, who made the time to meet with me in Los Angeles when I was looking for inspiration for my next powerful step to create value and impact in a new market. She took the time to listen to my story, and the advice she gave me is what I am giving you: believe in your brand, your vision, and the lifetime value you can give others. Step by step, people will start to take notice, and momentum will build. I walked out of our lunch date with a fire in my belly that I can and will do more to help others find their own superpower to fly high in business and life.

Jay Glazer, thank you for keeping me accountable on a daily basis while I wrote this book in Kamalaya and checking in from the US to make sure I remained on track. You showed me that we are all "unbreakable."

To the women in our Powerful Steps community—you light me up from the inside out. Your daily messages and posts of transformational moments you have experienced through the power of our programs and community are a true gift I cherish. Always remember: when you believe you can, you will.

To the A-Team who made it all happen: Nick Krull, my Creative Director for close to two decades helping me create brands I am proud of—TORSTAR and Powerful Steps. Thank you to the team at Mango—Hugo, Geena, Minerve, Roberto, Robin—you are living proof that you can work from anywhere in the world and create magic that adds value to the lives of others. Jasmine Jonte, for activating my thoughts and translating them into powerful online programs; Hugo Johnstone-Burt, for filming our masterclasses in a way which I know creates impact when people deep dive into the online content to level up; Lacy Kirkland, for aligning with my vision and helping us bring it to life at the most perfect moment in time.

Throughout the journey of writing this book, there are many more people who made the impossible possible, as you need space to create and an environment where you can flourish and bring out the best you have to give. This is not easy when you are a mother, wife, friend, and person building a new global business built on daily touch points of personal connection with others. Sometimes you need more than twenty-four hours in a day to make the impossible possible, and that is where people step up to provide you with the support and platform to make a difference.

To my husband who believed in my journey from the start—thank you. Your unwavering support of our family and my ambitious goals is one of life's greatest gifts. Thank you for giving me the space to create and "be me."

To my daughter Bella: thank you for being the ultimate wingwoman and seeing the possibilities in every moment of life. Seeing you happy makes me happy, and that is how we ultimately attract the miracles of life.

Now it's over to you to dream big, think big and make the impossible happen...

Much love,
TORY xox

About the Author

Tory Archbold is the CEO and founder of Powerful Steps, an online community and platform for women making global impact. The business is driven by human connection, creating opportunities for leaders to find their ultimate power through a heart-led skill set and the power of strategic storytelling to add VALUE to the companies they lead or create. Tory's philosophy is not to box tick, rather to lead and disrupt in a way that allows her community to be seen, to be heard, and to shine.

Tory hosts the *Powerful Stories* podcast, where she shares her tips and tricks for leading a more powerful life and interviews others on the power of their own stories to shine a light for others. Each interview guest is an authentic connection made through the power of coffee dating around the world.

Tory was the founder of brand communications agency TORSTAR, Australia's most high profile brand and communications agency. TORSTAR didn't get its reputation from hype; the results were real. With her trademark passion and integrity, Tory led her team of twenty-two staff and ten freelancers to deliver award-winning work with the world's top-performing brands, celebrities, and influencers, including Zara, Nespresso, Seafolly, Sukin, and Victoria's Secret. Impressively, Tory's launch event for Zara in Sydney clocked over 22,000 people in attendance and was Zara's most successful retail launch event to date.

Tory believes in the power of human connection to create and deliver impact. She resides in Sydney, Australia.

Mango Publishing, established in 2014, publishes an eclectic list of books by diverse authors—both new and established voices—on topics ranging from business, personal growth, women's empowerment, LGBTQ+ studies, health, and spirituality to history, popular culture, time management, decluttering, lifestyle, mental wellness, aging, and sustainable living. We were named 2019 *and* 2020's #1 fastest growing independent publisher by *Publishers Weekly*. Our success is driven by our main goal, which is to publish high quality books that will entertain readers as well as make a positive difference in their lives.

Our readers are our most important resource; we value your input, suggestions, and ideas. We'd love to hear from you—after all, we are publishing books for you!

Please stay in touch with us and follow us at:

Facebook: Mango Publishing
Twitter: @MangoPublishing
Instagram: @MangoPublishing
LinkedIn: Mango Publishing
Pinterest: Mango Publishing
Newsletter: mangopublishinggroup.com/newsletter

Join us on Mango's journey to reinvent publishing, one book at a time.

CPSIA information can be obtained
at www.ICGtesting.com
Printed in the USA
JSHW030915050323
38476JS00009B/21

9 781684 811564